The Leap

* How 3 Simple Changes
Can Propel Your Career
from Good to Great

The
Leap

WITHDRAWN

Rick Smith

PORTFOLIO

PORTFOLIO
Published by the Penguin Group
Penguin Group (USA) Inc., 375 Hudson Street, New York, New York 10014, U.S.A.
Penguin Group (Canada), 90 Eglinton Avenue East, Suite 700, Toronto, Ontario,
Canada M4P 2Y3
(a division of Pearson Penguin Canada Inc.)
Penguin Books Ltd, 80 Strand, London WC2R 0RL, England
Penguin Ireland, 25 St. Stephen's Green, Dublin 2, Ireland
(a division of Penguin Books Ltd)
Penguin Books Australia Ltd, 250 Camberwell Road, Camberwell,
Victoria 3124, Australia
(a division of Pearson Australia Group Pty Ltd)
Penguin Books India Pvt Ltd, 11 Community Centre, Panchsheel Park,
New Delhi – 110 017, India
Penguin Group (NZ), 67 Apollo Drive, Rosedale, North Shore 0632, New Zealand
(a division of Pearson New Zealand Ltd)
Penguin Books (South Africa) (Pty) Ltd, 24 Sturdee Avenue,
Rosebank, Johannesburg 2196, South Africa

Penguin Books Ltd, Registered Offices:
80 Strand, London WC2R 0RL, England

First published in 2009 by Portfolio,
a member of Penguin Group (USA) Inc.

1 3 5 7 9 10 8 6 4 2

ISBN 978-1-59184-256-9

Printed in the United States of America
Set in Sabon
Designed by Vicky Hartman

This book is dedicated to you, the reader.

It is no accident that you are holding this book.
Your potential has been waiting for this day.
The time has come to explore an unexpected future,
to accomplish something beyond yourself,
to turn your career into a calling.

This is your invitation to stop working and start living.

· CONTENTS ·

The Leap

Introduction

The date was an unseasonably warm December 27, 2002, and I was sitting on an examining table, wearing a thin cotton gown, waiting for the doctor to return.

There was no urgency. This was my annual checkup, and in general, I felt perfectly healthy despite the five extra pounds I had lugged in with me. When my doctor, a balding man with an Uncle Fester look about him, finally made it back to the examining room with my test results, he gave me a reassuring smile and said, "Good news, Rick, you are completely unremarkable!"

I suppose I should have been thrilled at that moment. Bad things begin to happen to people even in their midthirties, and I had been spared such drama. Instead, I remember studying the regular ups and downs of my EKG and thinking with a sigh, gee, this is what unremarkable must look like. Time goes by at a steady pace. There's the occasional blip, but in the end one page looks eerily similar to the next.

In fact, my EKG results seemed at that moment to be a tracking line for my own career, unfolding along a flat line all the way to the horizon. I was a middle-class striver—luckier than some, unluckier than others, but just mostly average for the type. I was, in a word, ordinary, as rut-stuck as I could be, and I couldn't see any way out of the fix.

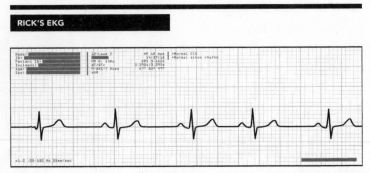

My heart EKG at age 35, but as I stared at the paper, all I could see was the trajectory of my life. Certainly an occasional bit of excitement and hope, but for the most part flat-line, blip, flat-line—as far as my eyes could see.

Welcome to the future, I thought to myself as the doc clapped me on the back and told me to get dressed. Welcome to more of the same.

Then, something completely unexpected happened: My job blew up, my life turned on a dime in an extraordinary new direction, and my energy level and life EKG (not my heart one, thank goodness) jumped right off the page. Over the course of the next 18 months, I wrote a best seller, founded a company that brought me into close contact with some of the leading thinkers and personalities of our time, and eventually sold it for more money than I ever dreamed I might make in my lifetime.

And as all this unfolded, I kept wondering how in the heck this had happened to, of all people, me. And how many others are there like me—men and women who have busted free from utterly ordinary trajectories to accomplish extraordinary things with their lives?

That's where my search began. I set out to find people who had achieved great success without being gifted with the talents and drive that might have marked them as special from an early age. What were the common threads among these extraordinary "ordinary" people? Why had their careers gone in a different direction than those of men and women with almost identical circumstances and resources who did indeed seem to be bogged down in the ordinariness of the everyday? What helped these extraordinary people break loose, and what can the rest of us—those who are stuck in average—learn from them?

This book is where my quest has led me, the culmination of half a decade of intensive interviewing and research. Along the way I have met dozens of remarkable people, and I have been incredibly fortunate to have them share their stories with me. I've also taken a journey into the brain and the interplay of thought and emotion so I could better understand why so many of us are reluctant to let go of lives that neither utilize our strengths nor engage our passions.

What I have discovered is dramatic, counterintuitive, and, for the reader, potentially life changing. The fact is, the woods are full of ordinary people, everyday Joes and Janes, who have transformed rut-stuck careers into deeply fulfilling callings—work that not only has brought them great personal satisfaction but has also had a great and lasting impact on others.

These aren't cases of people who "fixed" their weaknesses.

Rather, they became more fully and completely themselves. Nor are these people who dared great things. Instead of courting risk, they eliminated it from the equation of their careers and thus helped to assure their ultimate success. Nor, finally, did these men and women wear themselves to the bone with exceptional effort; in every instance, they simply rode the momentum of an exceptional idea.

Best of all, I've learned that these leaps are replicable. They follow a pattern, a set of steps that has been ingraining itself in our thinking since the prehistory of the species.

The Leap is a guide to personal evolution. It's a "good to great" manual for individuals, a book about aligning passions and skills, and about the amazing energy that gets released when we find our personal "sweet spot." All of us have a special place on the spectrum where the best of our ability intersects with what most inspires us. Too few of us ever find that spot or even know it's there. But it is there, and it's magic. This book will point you to it.

In these pages, you will read about the power of certain ideas to cut through all the filters, spam, and otherwise that our brains have erected in an age of total-saturation communication. All ideas are not created equal. Some are force multipliers: they have the power to engage others in your quest and assure that you do not leap alone. I will show you why that is so and how to take advantage of it.

Reimagining your career and reigniting your potential takes work, sometimes enormous effort. The forces that hold us in our present circumstances are many and powerful. Yet, as the title suggests, this is not a guide to living and acting on the edge. In fact, this is a book about *predictability*, a book about using the hardwiring of the brain to assure that, whatever change you set out to make in your career, the odds will be stacked in your favor.

The Leap is not a call to toss aside all that you've already achieved in your career. But it does ask that you find the courage—and it does take courage—to open yourself up to the possibility of a future of great impact, rich with fulfillment. Many have found this within the walls of their current employers, or even within their current roles. If you can do the same, both you and your employer will be the better for it.

Most of all, this is a book about real people. Some have become almost household names; others have succeeded more quietly as teachers, community leaders, corporate innovators, inner-city mission workers, and rock promoters. But what they have in common with each other is how ordinary they all were at the outset. They faced the same challenges and fears as most of us. They were saddled with the same flawed tool set most of us are born with, and yet they did break out. Rather than hold them back, the very fact of their ordinariness propelled them forward. This book will show you why and how that was so, and how the same thing can happen to you.

I call the place where so many are stuck today a "rut" not just because it's a familiar metaphor. A rut is *exactly* what that feels like. Try as hard as you might, you can't steer your way out or, worse, the wheels just spin in place. Either way, the direction is set, your career trajectory predetermined. Yesterday and today and tomorrow are all one and the same.

And I call the process you will discover in this book—the one that pulls you out of the rut—the "leap" because I have been through it and spent so many days talking with others who have done the same, and we all agree that at the moment you let go of your old trajectory, it is as if the normal rules of gravity have been suspended. You can call the moment of release—that inflection point in the journey from good to great—anything you want. Words in the end don't matter. The landing spot is yours alone. It's the journey that counts—that's where real clarity lies. That's where your future begins.

Work doesn't have to be just another four-letter word, and ordinary is neither a curse nor a life sentence. Good is not the enemy of great; it is the starting point to great fulfillment if we only let it be so.

Above all else, remember this: the ruts we may feel stuck in are largely of our own making. What we have built we can also undo. What we can dream we can achieve.

Of all this, I am Exhibit No. 1.

"Great Work, You're Fired!" 1

I grew up in a 30-by-30-foot brick house in Harrisonburg, Virginia, a sleepy town of 15,000 people nestled in the foothills of the Shenandoah Valley. My parents didn't have a lot of money, and too much of what extra they had got gobbled up by my ridiculously bad eyesight. By age two, I was already being fitted for glasses, which I promptly ruined. Other disasters followed until my parents settled on military-like plastic frames with a giant rubber nose protector and lenses thick enough to suggest deep-space exploration.

Needless to say, such singular eyewear did not promote popularity, but I survived, if mostly on the margins. My high-school grades were just good enough to get me into a solid public university, and my parents had just enough spare money left to help me pay the freight.

After college, I held a succession of jobs as a consultant, but the toll of my extensive travel became crystal clear one Saturday morning when my two-year-old daughter, the oldest of what are now three children, woke me with this memorable greeting: "Daddy, Daddy, thanks for coming to visit!" I called my employer that weekend and resigned. Thus, only a few months before my doctor pronounced me "completely unremarkable," I found myself on Employer No. 4, this time as an executive recruiter.

As had been the case with my consulting positions, I was competent at the work, and my firm, Spencer Stuart, was one of the tops in the business. But I clearly was no standout. By the time I had been with Spencer Stuart two years, the writing on the wall was hard to miss. I might make partner some day if I kept my nose ever to the grindstone. But my talents were average, and it would be a long slog to get there if I ever did.

Worse to me by far, I had no real zeal for the work. One day bled into the next, one task into another. Ever since childhood, I had been blessed with a naïve optimism that always led me to ask, "Why not?" Now, the question was getting whittled down to a single word: "Why?"

In short, I didn't know where I was going, and I was working like hell to get there. Sound familiar?

Did He Say "Severance"?

Studies don't always support what we intuit to be true, but in this case there's plenty of literature to show that where I found myself was common ground for a great many of us.

Since 1997, Gallup, Inc., has been tracking the workplace satisfaction of millions of employees. On average, Gallup has found that only about 30 percent of all workers are "engaged": they want goals so they can meet and exceed them; they're curious about the enterprise generally. Another 55 percent are what Gallup calls "not engaged": they've got a wait-and-see attitude about their jobs, their employers, and their coworkers.

And then there are the roughly 15 percent who are actively disengaged. Gallup refers to them by the semi-acronym "cave dwellers," where "cave" stands for Consistently Against Virtually Everything. Not only are they unhappy on the job, they're busy acting out their unhappiness by tearing down the positive accomplishments of their coworkers.

I was never a disruptive force at Spencer Stuart, and I was certainly never actively disengaged as Gallup defines the term, but I would have to say that "not engaged" captured me to a tee. I came, I saw, but I was never going to conquer. And then I had an inspiration. If my "day job" wasn't bringing me the satisfaction I wanted, maybe a night-and-weekend job would.

I was a voracious reader of business-themed books, everything from the autobiographies of corporate titans to futuristic visions of what the workplace would be like decades out to nuts-and-bolts manuals on how to increase sales, revenues, efficiency, you-name-it. For a number of years, I had been thinking that what would be really useful would be a book that explored the commonalities among highly successful people. I had stuffed several boxes with articles on the subject, and Spencer Stuart had a treasure trove of resources, so I thought, why not do it myself? And with that, some of my old optimism began to flow back into me.

I convinced my friend and fellow recruiter Jim Citrin to join me in the project, and we set out to write an introduction and an outline of what was to follow. Like most other professionals who aspire to see their names in print, I was completely in the dark about the challenges of actually getting a book published, but I knew that I needed this dream in my life as a counterbalance to my daily reality. And, in fact, the dream didn't die. In August 2003, *The 5 Patterns of Extraordinary Careers* first appeared in bookstores. Then to our utter and complete amazement, the book took off.

Encouraged by my CEO to hit the publicity trail, I did radio, television, and magazine interviews, published articles excerpting the book, and spoke in front of thousands. And while Spencer Stuart was never far from my mind and often mentioned in my presentations, not once in all that time did I think, "Boy, I can't wait to get back to head-hunting."

By November, three months after publication, we had climbed onto the *Wall Street Journal's* top-15 list of business best sellers. *Business Week* had us at No. 7, Amazon.com at No. 4. BN.com, the online e-tailer for Barnes & Noble, would eventually rank us No. 1 among career best sellers for 40-plus weeks.

For me, this was incredibly heady stuff. I all but jumped up and clicked my heels that November when Spencer Stuart's CEO—the same one who had sent me out on the book tour—called and said, "This has been great for the firm. In return, we really want to take care of you. Come see me and we'll discuss where to take your career next."

A private meeting to discuss my career? Forget the old rut. As I flew from Atlanta to the company's New York headquarters, I couldn't help but wonder what might lie ahead. A raise? A promotion? Perhaps he even wants me to run a small part of the business . . . like, say, *Europe*!

When I stepped into the CEO's office, his first words to me were, "Rick, what have you liked most about the last several months of your career?" To me, this was a slow hanger right over the center of the plate. I swung hard and launched into an excited description of my new life as a successful author. Forty-two minutes later he cut me off.

"Wow, Rick, your passion is amazing—this clearly seems to be your calling. But . . ." and with that he hesitated, "I must note that during this conversation you *never* mentioned head-hunting." He paused again, picked up one of the firm's recruiting-services brochures, and slid it across the table in front of me. "And in case you've forgotten, Rick, that's basically what we do."

In my memory the rest of the meeting flies by as a kind of static-filled blur. I recall words and phrases far more than whole sentences: "want to be supportive . . . innovative ideas . . . your first sponsor . . . personal introduction for you."

At one point along the way, I remember my heart sinking: had I played this one incorrectly? Yet as the meeting concluded and I headed to the elevator, I was still excited. The CEO had said something about my having personal access to his own Rolodex. This could be my big break!

Not until the elevator doors were sliding shut did I recall the boss's exact parting words: "In fact, we are so supportive, that we will even give you severance."

Severance?!

By the time I reached the first floor, it had finally sunk in that I had just been fired. Here I was, the coauthor of a best-selling book on career success, and my own career had just crashed and burned.

Birth of an Idea

I let that reality sink in for a day or two. Then I did what every mature, together, resilient person in the same circumstance would surely do. I PANICKED!

For starters, I immediately brushed off my resume, reviewing and rewriting it over and over again. I checked out job boards on the Internet and browsed the want ads in the newspaper. Ironically enough, I even went to bookstores and purchased several guides to career success.

The weeks passed with no job offers, but my mounting spare time also gave me space to nurture an idea that had first occurred to me while I was on my book tour. In the course of researching and writing about successful executives, I had been struck by the explosive growth of networking groups. Hardly a week passed that didn't include at least one invitation to me and just about everyone I knew to join some group or another. What's more, the groups clearly had a positive influence on career success. Peers helping peers just made sense. But I also was increasingly struck by the fact that none of these networking groups seemed to involve the very top executives, the most respected professionals in their fields, the highest-ranking person in their role in their company.

Why, I wondered? And what could I do about it? By then, my rejections had mounted high enough to cut a wide swath of free time, so I started to put pen to paper and draft a plan.

The idea was this: I would create the most influential network of top-level executives in the world—or more accurately, the most influential family of networks. Each network would consist of the 50 most important chief marketing officers,

CFOs, heads of human resources, and the like from not only around the nation but around the globe. Under the auspices of the umbrella organization I was going to create, these executives would meet periodically to share, debate, and collaborate on their most critical issues, and each of these executives would pay me tens of thousands of dollars per year just to join and participate.

I even came up with a name that seemed to capture the spirit and grandeur of the concept: World50, or w50 for short. I remember thinking more and more convincingly each day that maybe this is *it*, my way out! And it sure seemed as if it would be a lot more fun than working at some place that wasn't wild about my even being there.

That left only one small problem, the same one I had initially faced with my book: I hadn't a clue how to make all this happen.

Well, make that *two* problems. My wife and friends thought I was nuts, likely shell-shocked from being newly middle aged and suddenly unemployed. If w50 were such a great idea, certainly it would have already been done. Not to mention certain gaps in my own track record to date. Who was I, after all, to attempt to pull off something so audacious?

Only mildly deterred, I hosted a dinner of some of the smartest businesspeople I knew and pitched the idea to them, certain they would see the glimmer of genius within. Alas, they were unimpressed. Maybe I picked the wrong restaurant.

Slightly more discouraged, I put together a six-page Power-Point presentation and sent it to a top management consultant and former mentor whose opinion I greatly respected. Of all the people I knew, surely *he* would get it! But instead of providing the affirmation I was so desperately seeking, he responded with the devastating suggestion that I might want to focus on something "more realistic."

Maybe I *was* crazy, or just grasping at straws rather than facing the fact that I had been cast out to the cold, cruel exile of out-of-work professionals. Certainly, I was getting poorer by the day and no closer, it seemed, to any solution.

"Where Do I Sign Up?"

Spencer Stuart had generously allowed me to continue using my office for a couple months to conduct my job search, but that grace period was quickly coming to an end. In my last week there, I hauled in a dozen cardboard boxes and started packing up my things. I can recall reaching for the pile of research, notes, and documents that summed up my idea for World50 and worrying that if I packed this idea in the bottom of the box, I'd never take it out again. But that's just what I did. I put the documents in the box and piled more stuff on top. When I finally taped the box shut, it felt almost like a funeral.

Then I noticed a business card that had dropped to the floor. It came from Carl Gustin, the chief marketing officer of Eastman Kodak, whom I had met on a plane about seven years earlier. I was sure Carl wouldn't remember me, but just seeing his card lying there was like a revelation. I had sought opinions from everyone under the sun about this new business idea I had, but I had never once reached out to someone who actually might be a customer.

I decided to e-mail my six-page summary to Carl—he was still Mr. Gustin then—along with the request that we meet sometime within the next several months to discuss it.

One hour later, a return message from Carl popped into my e-mail inbox. I stared at it, unopened, for a long minute, the way high-school seniors stare at the envelopes waiting to tell them whether they have been accepted at the college of their choice. Was the envelope thick or thin? Then, taking a deep breath, I highlighted Carl's message and clicked on "read."

> Rick:
>
> I am involved in many groups like this.
> However, I know of nothing like this in terms
> of scope and scale, and think other marketing
> executives will find it incredibly valuable.
> Where do I sign up?!
>
> Carl

I must have sat motionless in my chair for an hour, reading the e-mail over and over like someone checking his lottery ticket to ensure it was the winning number. Not only did I finally have the glimmer of validation for my idea that I had so desperately hoped for, but I might have just landed my first customer.

A day later, I received a call at my home office.

"Hello, this is Rick," I said.

"Oh, my, I am so sorry to bother you, Mr. Smith. This is Ruth with accounts payable at Eastman Kodak, and I was looking for someone in w50's accounting department."

I covered the phone receiver with my left hand and let my arms drop to my lap. *Accounting department! What? I am World50's only employee. Wait a minute—what am I talking about? The company doesn't even exist yet?!*

"That's, okay, Ruth," I finally managed to stammer. "I'm happy to pass along a message."

"Well, we have been told we need to make a payment to World50 but can't seem to find the invoice. Can you have them fax us a copy?"

Again, the phone dropped to my lap. *I don't even know what an invoice looks like!*

That night, I created my first invoice ever, for $50,000—an amount that signaled the exclusivity of the membership, nearly twice the fee of other networking groups. After that, I stayed up the rest of the night designing the company's first logo. In the morning, I mailed the document off to Eastman Kodak, literally hot off the printer.

A Kid in Candy Land

In truth, everything concrete about w50 began from that moment. Two months later I had contacted 16 of the most influential marketing executives in the world, and all but one of them had agreed to join. The first group was filled and sold out within six months, with 50 executives each paying $50,000 to belong.

With this initial momentum, I recruited a talented and experienced staff and attracted even more influential people to join our advisor network. I enlisted the support of senior executives at some of the world's most respected professional services companies: Accenture, Omnicom, Bain, WPP, Gallup, and others. Collectively, they contributed hundreds of thousands of dollars in intellectual capital and branding and public relations support as well as making critical introductions to member prospects. And all of them—or their companies—actually *paid me* for the opportunity to help my fledgling business grow.

Soon I was launching other exclusive groups to fulfill the vision of a family of business communities and receiving overwhelmingly positive responses from each group. By then, the company was clearly an unequivocal success, by any measure.

Within two years of coming up with the idea of w50, I could tick off dozens of globally recognizable names with whom I had spent time conversing about business, government, and favorite causes: Jack Welch, Alan Greenspan, Martha Stewart, Earvin "Magic" Johnson, former U.S. Senate leaders Bob Dole and George Mitchell, Lance Armstrong, Richard Branson, and U2's Bono, among them. Robert Redford invited me and my team to spend a long weekend at his house. One memorable evening, Francis Ford Coppola poured me wine from his private cellar as he shared his secrets on creativity.

Throughout it all, I was much like a kid in Candy Land. I couldn't believe this was happening to me! But the fact is, I had accomplished what almost no one thought possible. I'd put together one of the most influential business networks in the world. And in the process, I had made a leap from the ordinary to the extraordinary.

Force Multipliers

The energy that founding w50 had released in me was astounding. Sixty-hour weeks flew by as if they were half that long. Challenges that would have loomed like mountains in my old, stuck life were suddenly reduced to relative molehills. Simply put, I couldn't wait to get out of bed in the morning. Better still, I knew I wasn't going to come home in the evening too dead tired and down in the dumps to enjoy spending time with my wife and kids.

I was successful, yes, beyond my wildest dreams. But after so many years of slogging down the same old path, I was finally fulfilled. And that made more of a difference than all the markers of success I could have possibly surrounded myself with.

A Quest for Understanding

How had it happened? And why? I had no experience as an entrepreneur. I didn't even want to be an entrepreneur! I had no business plan, and the outline I did cobble together was shot down as ridiculous by nearly everyone whom I respected. What's more, I had no seed money to get my idea off the ground. Still, my life had turned on a dime in a direction of success that no one, including myself, could have predicted or even imagined. As much as I was enjoying my newfound life, I felt an urgent need to understand what could have possibly allowed this to occur.

Some of the contributing factors seemed clear from the outset. The idea for my company's proposed mission—to provide influential managers around the world with a forum for peer exchange—had tapped a need in the marketplace that was not being served. That's straight out of Business 101. I was supplying a service that didn't previously exist and for which there was great pent-up demand.

I also hadn't ventured far from my area of expertise. As a management consultant and executive recruiter, I had been exposed at the margins to the sort of top-level executives who were rapidly becoming my clientele. That's not to say I was on anyone's radar screen before I launched w50—I definitely was not—but it wasn't as if I had cast over my old day job completely to become a professional tango dancer.

Now that I was running a highly successful business, everyone was quick to cast me in the role of the ballsy, lone-wolf entrepreneur—the kind who throws caution to the wind and bravely charges forward against all odds. I liked the thought of myself as a kind of biz-oriented Evel Knievel, but I also knew that wasn't the case. I hadn't dived into this new life. Truth be told, I was scared to death of risk, and I resisted change, *any change*, nearly every step of the way. I even continued interviewing for a *real job* well after I had received checks from my first customers.

What's more, I hadn't gotten where I was on my own effort, or anything like it. Dozens of people had joined me in my quest, without any direct obligation to do so. World50 had energized me as I had never been energized before, but I ultimately had been carried to my goal on a wave of other people's enthusiasm.

Thus it was that, almost with a sense of guilt, I boiled my search for answers down to one basic, three-part question:

How could someone who avoided significant risk, who never changed who he was, and who succeeded in great part through the efforts of others, have experienced such an incredible life transition?

That's where I concentrated, and that's where the answers were waiting.

Finding the Path

For starters, I revisited the extensive body of research I had conducted for *5 Patterns*, this time looking at it through a different lens. My own version of an extraordinary career had told me there was more to learn and fresh perspectives to factor in. From there, I branched out to explore the fields of biology, modern culture, psychology (including the relatively new branches of cognitive neuroscience, and neuroeconomics), physics, communications, sociology, animal behavior, and social networks. I even traveled to Berkeley, California, to get plugged into a brain-scanning machine.

I also just started talking about what had become my consuming interest, and once again, friends and even relative strangers began enlisting in the cause. It was truly amazing to me to discover how many of us know people who have lifted themselves up to new levels of achievement and fulfillment despite the old curse of being gifted with only (seemingly) average talents and resources.

A friend of a friend of my wife introduced me to Sara Blakely, a one-time fax saleswoman who launched Spanx, the women's clothing line that has taken off like a rocket over the last five years. By a route even more tenuous, I ended up having an incredible conversation with Brad Margus, a shrimp farmer turned renowned genetics expert. And so it went, from person to person and example to example.

I wasn't alone. Countless others, I came to learn, have defied a lifetime trajectory of ordinary and managed astounding accomplishments. What's more, like me, they didn't take reckless and unnecessary risks. They stayed true to who and what they were, and they benefited from legions of others who joined their cause. Most amazing to me, while the details of our journeys were always singular in the extreme, the patterns we followed were so similar as to form what amounted to a physical principle.

That's the real insight that my multiyear quest yielded: There is a path that almost all of us can follow to substantially improve the stature and trajectory of our life. By conscientiously applying the framework of ideas I have uncovered, it is possible to achieve a life of extraordinary impact and fulfillment beyond your most ambitious dreams.

That's where we begin: with the surprising, almost counterintuitive, yet well-trod path that can lead to great success and contentment, and with the old habits and beliefs, many grounded in the evolutionary development of the brain, that hold us back.

First I invite readers who want to move to a deeper level of engagement with this book to begin filling out the journal that follows and those at the end of subsequent chapters. "My Leap Journal"—named for the tipping point that will carry you from where you are to what you can become—will help prepare the way.

My Leap Journal—
"Great Work, You're Fired"

What is my ideal life? What are its elements? How would I describe it if it turned out exactly the way I wished?

Projecting my career on its current most likely trajectory to the point of retirement at age sixty-six or beyond, what have I accomplished? What are my proudest achievements? What are the things I wish I had done?

How different are the answers to Questions 1 and 2? Is the language, the terminology even the same? If not, why not?

What do I wish to accomplish that is unlikely given my current life trajectory? What am I willing to do to achieve it?

The Now Trap:
Stuck in the Status Quo

2

Our deepest fear is not that we are inadequate.
Our deepest fear is that we are powerful beyond measure.
It is our light, not our darkness that most frightens us.

— MARIANNE WILLIAMSON

At first glance, we humans would seem to be built for innovation and entrepreneurship. We're the species that dreams big things, the one that imagines a different future for ourselves, and it all begins with our neural architecture.

For 500 million years, the human brain (and the protohuman one that preceded it) did little more than poke along, not changing materially in size or shape. Then, beginning about 2 to 3 million years ago, our gray matter started to explode. Today, in what amounts to a wink in geological time, we have doubled our average brain volume from that benchmark break point.

But volume is the least of it. Cranial studies and other evidence show conclusively that what grew most dramatically in the brain over the last several million years was the frontal lobe, the part of the brain that allows us to visualize the future and anticipate coming events.

Today, we spend on average 12 percent of our time—3 hours each day, or roughly 10 years in an 80-year life span—contemplating what is to come. This is what makes us different from every other living thing: We live in the present but keep a foot in the past *and* the future.

Put another way, a cheetah or a great white shark or even our close DNA cousin the orangutan has to prove itself every day. We don't. We store up canned goods and water in case the power goes out; buy homes on time, via mortgages, in anticipation of rising values and future earning power; save money for our kids' college education so they can have a better a life than us; and invest in IRAs, Keoghs, and 401(k)s to help feather our own old age.

Torn Between Opposites

The planning-dreaming-poet side of the brain, the part that's ready to leap toward wherever opportunity might wait, is one facet. But there's another, older, survival-driven part of the brain that works in almost exact opposition.

Encouraged by our huge new frontal lobe, we envision big things to come, but when push comes to shove, our older brain fights like mad to defend the current state of our lives. We court risk in our imagination, then run from it in our daily lives. We are almost compelled to plot out alternative story lines for our lives and careers and families, but we are compelled even more powerfully to avoid what we imagine. That's the great irony of humankind: we are at once the animal capable of dreaming and the one that holds itself back from achieving its dreams.

True, we *are* wired to think about the future, but in critical ways, we are wired to think about it incorrectly.

An example: while our frontal-lobe-heavy brain structure focuses our attention on an abstract future, it doesn't give us much help in envisioning it as fundamentally different than the present. We might imagine ourselves in a new home or with a new job, or perhaps even in a new country or with a new spouse, but when the imagination can't supply all the pieces of the future puzzle, our brain fills in the missing spaces with images from the present—with what we see and know and feel every day.

Tattoo parlors, among other businesses, depend on this dead space between the future and present for customers. We know, or like to think, that we will always be in love, but if we could imagine that it wouldn't always be with "Tiffany," would we be nearly so likely to have her name emblazoned on our bicep? I don't think so.

(This tendency works in reverse as well. When we're missing a piece in our memories, we supply the answer from current experience, one large reason why siblings sometimes harbor such radically different versions of common events in their past.)

Imagining the Future to Avoid It

Psychologists refer to this cluster of phenomena as "presentism," and presentism has a profound effect on preserving and defending the status quo. Were we able to visualize our ultimate potential free of the present, we would be far more likely to pursue it. But because we are wired instead to define the future in terms borrowed from our present circumstances, we are likely to think that a leap to a fresh life trajectory ultimately will land us pretty much where we began. Why bother if we're simply going to be in a new office with a different title on the door, facing the same old exhausting frustrations?

Stuck in the present, we fret over how far up the corporate ladder we can climb, whether we will ever make VP of Sales, or what our compensation will be a dozen years out, when we really need to be asking ourselves what we should be doing with the rest of our lives. If we're not fulfilled, if we're not in touch with what we intuit our potential to be, the rest—titles, offices, salary—is all window dressing and empty calories.

The frontal lobe speaks loudly enough in our private daily counsels that we all know this to be true to some extent. We long for the change that will make us fully in touch with our essential selves. We ache for work that will leave us fulfilled and content. But the rest of our brain, conditioned by millions of years of human and prehuman experience, anticipates failure, not success. And because it does, it sends a very different message: The upside of dramatic change isn't worth the effort and exposure involved.

In effect, we imagine the future not so we can embrace it, but so we can avoid it.

Buying into Your Own Status Quo

Because we cling so tenaciously to the status quo, we also tend to overcommit to our present circumstances, overdefend the decisions that got us there, and overestimate the risk and costs of altering them.

Consider, for example, that annual sporting and betting extravaganza known as "March Madness," the NCAA Division I basketball championships. The more time you spend puzzling out all the brackets and possible combinations of Sweet Sixteen, Elite Eight, Final Four, etc., the more committed you become to your own predictions. If you then place a bet on the final outcome—and the FBI estimates $2.5 billion gets wagered each year—the odds are extraordinarily high that neither love nor money could get you to change your mind, at least until the first round has been played.

In effect, you have created a status quo and bought into it; studies have consistently shown that the bigger the bet and the more you fretted over it, the more certain you are that your reasoning is sound and the outcome you have predicted is highly likely. That's the way the brain works. It makes us sweat and strain over our decisions like a crew of ditchdiggers; then, once the decision is made, the brain invokes a psychological defense clause that says, Well, that sounds like a great bet to me. I'll stick with it through thick and thin.

So it is with jobs and careers and even life patterns. We often invest so heavily in them, and buy into the logic of our investment and decision making so thoroughly, that we see abandoning them at the one extreme as a kind of psychological suicide and at the other as an unnecessary dare, given that the future (as our flawed brains paint it) is so likely to re-create the present. Rather than face up to the potential of positive, dramatic change, we silence the argument within ourselves, and in doing so, we spare ourselves the pain both of a difficult contemplation and of potentially realizing that our assumptions about the future have been fundamentally flawed.

In various branches of science, this is known as a closed system. In more everyday terms, it's like walking into a dead-end alley. Maybe instead of calling it presentism, we should think of it as the "Now Trap." What *is* closes in around us. What *could be* seems impossibly distant. And the space between them appears far too risky to navigate. No wonder our personal ruts seem so hard to escape—they *are*, in fact, Now Traps every one.

Simply put, we are motivated more by the fear of losing what we have than we are by the possibility of gaining something of equal or greater value. Economists and psychologists have both shown that we expect losing a dollar to have much more impact than gaining a dollar. Even when the gain side of the equation is dramatically increased, the fear doesn't go away. Most of us would refuse a bet with an 85 percent chance of doubling our life savings because the big gain doesn't compensate us for the much smaller chance of losing it.

Psychologists have long assumed that terrible events such as violent crime have lasting negative effects on their victims, and sometimes they do. But more recent studies have found that most people who go through such traumatic experiences suffer relatively low levels of sadness for relatively brief times, then get on with life. The same is true with our work lives. We consistently overestimate how bad a job change or even a career shift will make us feel and how long we will feel that way, and thus we opt for what is, rather than for what could be. And yet for most of us, the emotional system is on the whole far more elastic than the brain will let us believe.

The Contrast Principle

One more item to factor into this status quo–cleaving Now Trap is something known as the Contrast Principle, which holds that we make judgments not against constant standards but largely through comparison. If, for example, we are presented with a series of photos of people with horrible muscle tone, then asked to evaluate our own physical condition, we will give ourselves far higher marks than if we have first been given a series of photos of people who are top physical specimens. Our condition is unchanged, our muscle tone is what it is, but our perception of it alters as the basis of comparison changes.

All that is only natural. We navigate the world via similes and metaphors. Unfortunately, though, in making judgments via contrasts, we selectively look to the extremes and thus tend to overestimate the differences involved. In effect, we clear out the middle, and push all comparisons out to the edge.

The late comedian George Carlin depicted this phenomenon dead-on in one of his famous quips: "Ever notice that anyone going slower than you is an idiot, but anyone going faster is a maniac?" Of course!

Studies have shown, for example, that 96 percent of cancer patients believe they are in better health than the average cancer patient, while logic and the rules of math tell us that only a nano-fraction fewer than 50 percent can be better than the average. At the other extreme, we assume that those whom the media celebrate as beautiful, innovative, entrepreneurial, highly intelligent, and so on are not just marginally more beautiful, innovative, entrepreneurial, and highly intelligent than us but massively so.

In some instances, they really are. Many would agree that Einstein was light-years smarter than the average Joe. In most cases, though, what we perceive to be a yawning chasm between us and those who have achieved extraordinary lives and careers is not nearly so formidable.

In the words of Nelson Mandela (and the continuation of the wonderful quote that opens this chapter): "We ask ourselves, 'Who am I to be brilliant, gorgeous, talented, fabulous?' Actually, who are you not to be?"

Roads Not Taken

These are the pranks the brain plays on us. This is the way it builds the Now Trap that holds us in the ruts of our lives and careers. The brain provides us with a massive frontal lobe to imagine the future, then tricks us into believing that whatever lies out there for us will not be all that different than the present. The brain gifts each of us with enormous potential, then convinces us that the risk of pursuing our potential is greater than the reward of achieving it. It allows us to envision what we might become, then tells us we lack the talent and skills to get there.

We can't help longing after the choices not made, the roads not taken, more than the choices we do make and the roads we do take. That again is part of what being a human being is all about. We're the decision-*making*, decision-*regretting* animal; we have the capacity to rue as well as to anticipate and to envision alternative futures for ourselves. But unlike the poet Robert Frost, we can't quite bring ourselves to take those roads less traveled, the ones that make, in Frost's words, "all the difference."

Our psychological immune system *is* poised to jump. It *wants* us to make the Leap. It can deal far more easily with too much courage than with too much cowardice. It's more comfortable with our stumbling forward than with our hedging our bets. But the brain won't let us do that without a fight that most of us are not prepared to make.

Thus we wage psychological warfare on ourselves. But—and this is the critical point—*we don't have to*. The Now Trap is formidable, but it's not Houdini proof. We simply have to start looking at life through a different lens, and perhaps more than anyone I know, Sara Blakely points the way to what that lens should be.

From Fax to Feetless Panty Hose

One humid summer morning was pretty much like another one for Sara Blakely. For half a decade she had been pulling her aging Honda into small office complexes and parking. Dressed in a blouse, pants, and an uncomfortable pair of control-top panty hose—a requirement of Danka Office Imaging, her employer—Sara would open the trunk, haul out a heavy fax machine, and eye the stretch of hot asphalt and maybe a flight of stairs that stood between her and her next potential sale. Then, with a sigh, she would cradle the fax machine in her arms and set of on yet another day on the job.

"The work was quite exhausting, emotionally and physically," remembers Sara, "but I had one advantage. I was one of the only people who didn't quit." Indeed, Sara's persistence led her eventually to become one of the top salespeople in thecompany. But the cost of success was high: her boss was a screamer and the quotas were insane. This was never what she wanted for herself.

Since age five, Sara had wanted to be a trial attorney. She loved to debate and convince people she was right, and in the movies and TV shows she watched, that's just what trial attorneys did. Sara entered the University of Florida in 1989, convinced that she was on a straight track to law school and beyond. After her sophomore year, she transferred to Florida State to be near a new boyfriend, but her determination to be a lawyer never wavered. Then, not long after graduation, her dream hit a roadblock.

"I flunked the LSAT," Sara says. "Well, you can't really flunk it, but that's certainly what it felt like."

With her lifelong goal derailed, Sara set her sights on a somewhat different ambition: she applied for the role of Goofy at Disney World. But, alas, even this dream turned elusive. Disney had very strict height requirements for the role of Goofy, and Sara didn't measure up. If she wanted to work at the world's most famous theme park, she would have to settle for the far less prestigious role of a chipmunk.

"It was quite depressing. I could reconcile myself to not becoming the lawyer I had always dreamed about. But to be sweating around in a chipmunk suit all summer was a tough pill to swallow. I mean, was Goofy really too much to aspire for?"

Sara soon fled Disney for the sales job with Danka and took to it quickly, but although she was soon making nearly $60,000 a year—more than many of her friends—the job held little interest for her and offered absolutely no fulfillment apart from the paycheck. To escape, Sara tried a number of visualization exercises, hoping to discover some alternative future that might be available to her.

"I came up with two ideas. One, I could become a stand-up comic. The idea of standing in front of a crowd, trying to be funny, terrified me, but maybe that is what attracted me to it as well. The second thing I thought was that I could start my own business. Through my visualization exercises, I could clearly see myself being a successful leader and business owner, but I had no idea what product I could sell."

Rather than limit her dream to a single path, as she had done when she aspired to become a trial attorney, Sara decided to pursue both alternatives, without sacrificing her day job or jeopardizing the small stake she had managed to save from her earnings. Before long, she was doing open-mic nights at comedy clubs around the country, testing her talent and honing her skills. The experience, she says, was invaluable, but she never made a dime from her performances.

Simultaneously, Sara kept trying to envision how her business dream might play out. Who would she manage? What types of people would she hire? What would her leadership style be like? The questions were fine to play with, but they kept begging a larger issue: what kind of product or service was this imaginary business going to be making or supplying?

Then one Saturday in her apartment, Sara dove into her closet, getting ready for an evening out.

"I had purchased this wonderful pair of white pants that I wanted to wear," she says, "but I couldn't find anything to wear underneath that didn't show through. This wasn't the first time I had tried to do this. Ever since I bought the pants, I had been getting them out before some party or another, trying them on, then hanging them back up again. It was frustrating, and I guess I had finally had enough of it. I reached in my drawer for some scissors, cut the feet off of my control-top pantyhose—the kind Danka always made me wear—and when I put the pants back on, nothing showed through!

"I stood there wondering how many other women are out there right now with a great pair of white pants in their closet, unable to wear them. I can even remember getting angry that women had become slaves of uncomfortable fashion accessories, designed by a male-dominated industry. And that's when it hit me. We didn't have to be, and I could make it happen!"

"Is This Candid Camera*?"*

With that, a fashion empire was born, but it didn't happen overnight. Sara had never taken a business course. She knew nothing about patent law except that she needed to secure a patent for her feetless panty hose if she wanted to protect the idea. She had been in sales and soon would be transferring to become a sales trainer, but she had never even walked inside a manufacturing plant, and now she was contemplating a future in which she would be running one. And to get all this off the ground, she had a war chest of some $5,000, her life savings. She didn't even own a house that she could put up as collateral.

Sara tackled trademarks and patents in the local university library at night, after work. When she finally approached several local lawyers about securing her feetless panty hose patent, they found the idea so wacky that they actually asked her if she had been sent by *Candid Camera*. So Sara wrote the application herself, found a lawyer to help with the small stuff, and basically secured the patent on her own.

Sara even came up with a great name for her product—SPANX, a sexy wordplay that has the added advantage of drawing attention to the part of a woman's anatomy the product is most meant to flatter. That left her with the 800-pound gorilla in the business plan: manufacturing. She spent months researching hosiery mills online and then made several. calls, trying to find someone who would make a prototype for her, but to no avail. Half out of desperation, she took a week off work to push her idea in person.

"I drove all around North Carolina, begging mill owners to help make my idea. They always asked the same three questions: 'And you are . . . ?' 'And you are representing . . . ?' 'And you are financially backed by . . . ?' When I answered Sara Blakely to all three, they sent me away, not to mention they thought the idea 'made no sense, and would never sell.'

"Two weeks later I received a call from a mill owner who said he 'decided to help make my crazy idea.' When I asked why the change of heart, he said, 'I have two daughters.' Turns out they didn't think the idea was crazy at all."

"Follow Me to the Bathroom"

Now, she needed a customer.

"I thought, why not call Neiman Marcus; I liked to shop there. Everyone thought I was nuts to do that—Neiman Marcus is the place you go *after* you have already had some significant success. But I was naïve to the way things should be done, and there are numerous times when that has played completely to my advantage."

Sara used the cold-calling skills she had mastered at Danka to find her way to a buyer for Neiman Marcus and make her pitch in a hurry.

"I really don't think there is much to talk about," the buyer answered, "but hey, if you are willing to get on a plane and come here, I will give you 15 minutes."

Sara flew out to Texas with her feetless panty hose prototype stuffed in a ziplock bag and met the woman in a small room, one in a row of many such cubicles. After brief introductions, Sara told the buyer, "Look, I know we don't have much time, so I think you should follow me to the bathroom."

She took the somewhat startled woman's hand and off they marched to the ladies' room. "Look at my backside," Sara said as she first modeled her slacks with a pair of standard panty hose underneath. Then, she went into a stall, slipped off the ordinary panty hose and put on her own product instead, and returned.

"As I turned around to show her, the woman just stared without speaking. I didn't need to say anything. Then she finally reacted. 'Wow. I get it. I really get it. Let's talk about getting this in our stores immediately.'"

Months later, the first SPANX hit the shelves at Neiman Marcus. After that, Nordstrom, Saks, and Bloomingdale's fell like dominos. That's when, more than two years after her flash of entrepreneurial brilliance, Sara finally told Danka to find someone else to peddle fax machines.

Eventually, even Oprah Winfrey weighed in with an endorsement on her show. More eventually, Target called, asking Sara for an exclusive in-store brand—what became the thoroughly cheeky ASSETS. With that, history was made, and Sara had launched it all out of the back of her apartment with just about enough front money to buy a two-week vacation in Hawaii.

The Myths That Hold Us Back

Sara Blakely's story *has* to inspire. Once her business began to take off, there was no stopping her. Today, Spanx is a leading-edge women's clothing company with $250 million in annual sales. And Sara hasn't stopped there. In addition to being the founding CEO of her company, she also launched and now directs the Sara Blakely Foundation, which helps women around the globe with education and entrepreneurial ventures.

Sara has traveled widely, appeared frequently on TV, and become a go-to person for the business press. As I was writing this book, she was closing on a Manhattan town house overlooking Central Park so she wouldn't have to depend on hotels during her frequent trips to the Big Apple.

In fact, the markers of Sara's extraordinary success are everywhere, but what is more amazing—and to me, more telling—is just how ordinary she was before becoming so successful. She graduated right in the middle of the pack in high school, went to a state university, then transferred after two years to another one, not to upgrade her education but to follow her guy. The law-school admission test blew apart Sara's childhood ambition; Disney World wouldn't let her start any further up the ladder than a chipmunk's costume. At Danka, she began as an entry-level salesperson and remained there slogging it out for seven long, painful years.

Imagine Sara's life trajectory portrayed on a graph, with the x-axis (horizontal) representing time and the y-axis the life gauge, ranging from ordinary on the bottom to extraordinary at the top. For the first 25 years, the trajectory is practically a flat line hovering not far above ordinary. Sara strives, she hustles, she hauls her fax machines to office after office, and while her pay ascends, her happiness is clearly on hold. Maybe work isn't quite a four-letter word for her, but it's close to that.

Then something happens that imperceptibly begins to separate Sara's story from the common run. Frustrated by the rut she is stuck in and where she seems to be heading, Sara begins to visualize another future for herself—a future unconfined and undefined by the terms of her present circumstance. The line that represents her life's trajectory doesn't yet change

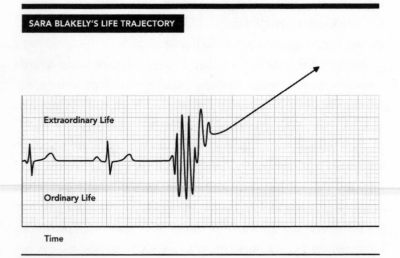

SARA BLAKELY'S LIFE TRAJECTORY

Extraordinary Life

Ordinary Life

Time

Like my own "Life EKG," Sara Blakely's trajectory was mostly unremarkable, until she made the Leap and it jumped straight off the page.

direction, but it is jagged now, filled with peaks and valleys as it skitters along the x-axis. And then, all of a sudden, there's ignition, and the line takes off, soaring up the y-axis.

Why? What does Sara's story tell us about that interim stage, about that critical inflection point between ordinary and extraordinary? For starters, it says that so many of the myths that hold us in the Now Trap and keep us stuck in the status quo are fundamentally wrong.

Myth 1: To make a great change in your life, you must change who you are.

Not so. SPANX didn't succeed so spectacularly because Sara Blakely consciously remade herself in the mold of a women's undergarment titan. SPANX became a great success precisely because pursuing the idea of feetless panty hose freed Sara to become even more her essential self.

She always had chutzpah—that's the one quality a would-be stand-up comedian can't be without. You need extraordinary nerve to walk into the spotlight in a comedy club and launch into your monologue. Those are tough audiences, if they pay any attention at all. With SPANX, she ratcheted the chutzpah up even higher and turned it to a larger cause.

Initially, Sara had no advertising budget, nor any money to advertise with, so she worked with what she had: nerve and guts. SPANX was no sooner on the Neiman Marcus shelves then Sara called all her friends and begged them to not just buy the product but to make a big to-do when they did. Her friends also helped her call newspapers, TV stations, and magazines all over the country to create the kind of buzz that would separate her product from the pack.

For over a year, Sara also did in-store rallies for sales associates, then hung around for the rest of the day to buttonhole potential customers as they came in. She became notorious, she says, for lifting up her pant leg to every woman who walked by.

In 2002, less than a year into full production, Sara received Ernst & Young's Entrepreneur of the Year award. Two years later, at the height of expanding her business, she took a three-month leave of absence to join Virgin Atlantic founder Richard Branson in a Fox TV show called *The Rebel Billionaire: Richard Branson's Quest for the Best.*

Even to her, the idea must have seemed a little off-the-wall, but as she traveled the globe with Branson and other participants, Sara developed a desire to help women around the world launch their own businesses. The Sara Blakely Foundation grew out of that experience, and the first seed money—$750,000—came form Richard Branson, his entire proceeds for taking part in the Fox show.

These are the sorts of things that happen not when we become someone else but when we align our innate passions and strengths to set free our own best selves. Sara was always a talented saleswoman, but other people's fax machines were never what she wanted to sell. Sara enjoyed getting people excited. She liked being on stage, but she knew that stand-up comedy was extremely unlikely to pay the bills. And she'd visualized running a successful business, leading and inspiring a team, but she didn't have a product.

Then she cut the feet off her panty hose, began to think about what she had done, and suddenly things fell completely into place. Now that Sara was selling something she was deeply passionate about, her ability to entertain and engage could lead to incredible attention for her product, and Sara could assume the leadership role she had always dreamed about.

Myth 2: To make a great change in your life, you must go it alone.

This is both the most debilitating of the myths and the most untrue. Who wouldn't find it daunting to leap alone? But as Sara Blakely's and my stories show—and as the stories of many other people you will meet in these pages confirm—going it alone won't get you there, except by the hardest route.

I'm sure Sara could not have predicted it as she headed into her leap, but she ultimately had a whole convoy traveling with her. Because feetless panty hose was such a simple product, everyone could "get it": the daughters of the hosiery mill owner who insisted to their father that hers was an idea long overdue; the first buyer at Neiman Marcus, who saw the same thing; the friends who drummed up publicity while Sara raised her pant leg from store to store; the legions of women with new pants staring frustratingly in the mirror; the many talented employees who joined Sara's team because they saw the potential for the product and the company but also because they, too, wanted to liberate women everywhere from the tyranny of the uncomfortable imposed by a male-dominated fashion industry; even Oprah Winfrey, Gwyneth Paltrow, and other celebrities who began talking up Sara's products after wearing them in some of the world's most glamorous venues.

To be sure, Sara worked tirelessly on behalf of the company, but something about this simple idea generated a wave of enthusiasm beyond anything that she could have accomplished on her own.

I can't claim anything like that star list. My guardian angels were mostly MBAs, not outtakes from the World's Most Admired People, but the practical effect was the same. Carl Gustin, the Eastman Kodak chief marketing officer, signed up when w50 was nothing but a few pages of paper; many others followed in his footsteps. By the time I started renting office space and hiring staff, I was flying as much on all their wings as I was on my own. Like Spanx, w50 became, without my ever intending it to be, a collaborative effort.

Myth 3: To make a great change in your life, you must take a great risk.

Think of this as the myth of the entrepreneur. A bold (verging on reckless) guy drops out of college to start a new business in his garage. He gets a second mortgage on the house and scrapes along taking risk after risk that would make us mere mortals queasy. Then, seemingly out of nowhere, he gets a break, wins the start-up lottery, and sells his company. Big risk pays off with big money.

Don't get me wrong. There are certainly examples of daring entrepreneurs whose lives actually follow this great risk–great reward story line. But here's a reality check: most don't! In fact, this is one of those situations in which all the built-in brakes of the human psyche do serve us well. The brain goes out of its way to let us know that jumping off a cliff with an untested parachute is not just a bad idea but a terrible one. And, in truth, you don't have to do that to make the sort of leap that can carry you to extraordinary success.

It took Sara Blakely a full year to secure a patent and nearly as long to find a small plant willing to manufacture a prototype. Her first sale was a cold call. In the end, she risked only $5,000 of her own money and never quit her job until the product was already a success in the market and she had such momentum propelling her forward that all she had to do was ride along with it.

No question about it: Sara today seems to exist on another plane altogether from those who would like to get where she is. But what is important to remember is where she began this incredible journey, how short the trip really was that got her to where she is today, and what minimal danger she exposed herself to along the way. In the next chapter, you will find out why that is so and how you can structure your own leap to assure that you (a) become not someone else, but more completely who you already are, (b) don't go it alone, and (c) avoid great risk.

My Leap Journal—
The Now Trap

What is it about my job that makes me feel trapped?

Am I willing to give myself permission to open up to new possibilities?

What is my Aspiration-to-Rationalization Ratio? (In other words, how much time do I spend dreaming of a brighter future versus defending my current state?) How has this changed over time? Do I really believe the arguments I am trying to sell myself?

Are there dreams that I previously determined were unrealistic that I should begin dreaming again?

Breaking Away: The Three Rules

3

Some men see things as they are and say, "Why?"
I dream of things that never were and say, "Why not?"

— GEORGE BERNARD SHAW

The one constant in life is change. Biologically, we don't have any choice in the matter: Bodies grow. Cells age. Hormonal infusions come and go. One day we are a new teenager bursting with energy. A wink in time later, we're bent with age. That's the cycle of life. If we live long enough to see it through, most of us manage to adjust gradually to the shifting terrain we inhabit.

Maybe because it arrives more serendipitously, career change—or the possibility of it—can be more unsettling than biological change. Something upsets our job status or reminds us of how unsatisfactory it is. A significant life alteration compels us to contemplate a major work change. Whatever it is that pushes us forward, we find ourselves nearing a ledge, eyeing the leap.

As we have just seen, the brain has a solution for times like these: don't! Its first line of defense is a bunker mentality—circle the wagons, pile up the sandbags, hunker down in the current rut, and see it through. All of that is understandable, especially in light of evolutionary experience. But as we also have just seen, the times that try us most and the life situations that seem the most intractable and troubling can also be our purest chances for liberation. As Francis Ford Coppola once told me, "The seeds of great success are often right in front of us, hidden in the ashes of adversity." It's not the situation, in short, that ultimately determines the real outcome; it's what we do with it—the change we open ourselves up to and the change we close ourselves off from.

"Pain is inevitable," an ailing friend told me the other day, "but despair is optional." I'll never forget that saying, and for me, Brad Margus will always be the person I think of first when I recall it.

Why Me?

On a drizzly afternoon in the fall of 1994, Brad and his wife Vicki sat quietly in a cramped doctor's office. For one of the rare times in his life, Brad wore a blue blazer over his jeans. Vicki wore a dark gray sweater. Their hands were clasped tightly together as they waited for the doctor to come in.

This wasn't their first consultation. A few years earlier, when their oldest son, Jarrett, was about 18 months old, Brad and Vicki had noticed that he seemed a bit clumsy—not all that strange for a growing, curious toddler, but as time passed, Jarret became more wobbly, not less.

"So we talked with the doctor," Brad remembers. "He said that maybe there wasn't enough oxygen in the womb for a few seconds when he was being delivered. 'He's not going to be an Olympic athlete,' the doctor said, 'but it won't get worse.'"

Brad and Vicki took comfort in that diagnosis. They didn't care about Olympians. They just wanted healthy, happy children. But then about a year later, while watching Jarrett play with his younger brother, Quinn, both parents noticed something that made them pause. Quinn was beginning to exhibit some of the same wobbly characteristics that Jarrett had shown. What were the odds that both brothers had suffered the same oxygen deprivation in the womb?

Thus began what seemed like an almost constant round of medical tests to determine what was affecting their boys, or at least to discover how to sufficiently treat their symptoms. Doctor after doctor had studied the test results, but no one had been able to offer them a reason, until this day.

Sitting with a new pediatrician in a tiny office behind a closed door, Brad and Vicki learned that their sons had ataxia-telangiectasia—A-T, for short—a rare inherited disease that gradually but inexorably brings about immune deficiency, neuron degeneration, cancer, and finally death. So rare was the disease, the pediatrician said, that not only was there no cure, there wasn't even any research going on to find one.

"That day," Brad recalled, "we began to mourn the deaths of our two sons, standing so seemingly healthy in front of us."

Rugged-looking, with a shock of thick brown hair, Brad might have been just about any man up to that moment. After college he worked a few years for a seafood company, then decided to move to Florida and start his own wholesale shrimp business. The work wasn't glamorous; shrimp farming wasn't something he felt called to do. But the business had struggled into profitability and was now steadily growing, and by his late twenties, Brad figured he was into shrimp farming for the long haul.

Now, Jarrett's and Quinn's terminal illness had upset all of Brad's expectations. He continued to lead his small company by day but spent his nights reading medical journals that he could barely understand, trying to understand a world that was utterly foreign to him.

"Sometimes it would take hours to get through a single paragraph," he says.

He eventually also took more direct action.

"We didn't know what to do, but rather than feel helpless to confront the situation, Vicki and I decided to set up a non-profit entity called the A-T Children's Project so that we could at least raise some money."

Brad and Vicki did manage to raise several thousand dollars for the cause, but once the money was in the bank, they realized they had no game plan for putting the funds to work. So, on a whim, Brad made a cold call to one of the most renowned scientists in the medical field and, after several hours, miraculously convinced him to chair the A-T Children's Project advisory board.

From there, with growing confidence, Brad was able to bring together doctors, scientists, research centers, and even pharmaceutical companies in the quest to find a cure for A-T and related diseases. Two years later, as a direct result of Brad's efforts and the support of his foundation, researchers were able to isolate and identify the gene linked to the A-T disorder.

The story, though, doesn't end there.

Brad's relationships and his positive reputation in the biotechnology industry eventually led to his cofounding and serving as CEO of Perlegen Sciences, a San Francisco Bay Area biotech pioneer. Under Brad's leadership, Perlegen developed the technology to map the individual human genome in a mere fraction of the time the process had previously taken.

As this book goes to press, A-T is still incurable, and Jarrett and Quinn Margus are slowly succumbing to their horrible disease. But despite the grim prognosis for his own children, Brad and his work have had a seminal impact on the emerging science of personalized medicine, changing the ways in which drugs are developed in the battle against disease.

In 2000, President George W. Bush appointed Brad his genetics expert on the National Advisory Neurological Disorders and Stroke Council. A few years later, California held a spectacular gala to celebrate passage of a historic, $3 billion research initiative in genetics. In attendance were world leaders, billionaires, Nobel Prize winners, and Brad Margus, who had been asked to deliver the keynote speech.

He began his speech with a simple question, "Why me?"

When Conventional Doesn't Fit

Why me, indeed. How was it that Brad Margus managed to make the leap to extraordinary achievement and improbable success?

If Brad's life ever was made into a biopic, the movie might well open with brief flashes of Jarrett and Quinn, and the wobbliness that first alarmed their parents, then cut to that wrenching moment in the pediatrician's office when Brad and Vicki learn about A-T. From there, the script would paint a picture of dramatic and sudden change as Brad set out on a life-or-death race for a cure to save his sons.

That's Hollywood, all right, but that's not really the way

it happened. Brad's nights were absorbed by medical journals because he felt compelled to understand, to do something, but he didn't immediately sell the shrimp farm and remake himself as a genetics philanthropist and entrepreneur. That happened years later. In fact, when he and Vicki set up their small foundation to raise money for research, they carefully labeled the initiative a "project," in part to convince themselves that it would not permanently alter their lives. Because they were scared to death, the impulse to grasp tightly to their previous lives was stronger than ever.

So was it Brad's ambition and drive to succeed that lifted him above the multitudes and stamped him as extraordinary? Certainly he has those qualities in abundance, but ambition and drive are not in short supply in the world today. Indeed, if ambition and drive alone could assure transformative action, the extraordinary would be nothing more than ordinary. Nor can ambition and drive alone explain how Brad accomplished so much in so little time, especially in an industry filled with tireless scientists and bold entrepreneurs.

Was it, then, the terrible threat to Brad's children that so motivated him and similarly inspired others to join his crusade? Brad would likely still be in the shrimp business today if his sons had remained healthy, but their diagnosis doesn't explain the wave of support that flowed Brad's way. While A-T is certainly an attention-grabbing and tragic disease, it is present in fewer than 500 children around the world at any one time. Everyone's heart goes out to this handful of children, but the pharmaceutical industry does not invest in potential cures for diseases that affect fewer than a million people, let alone fewer than 500.

How, then, does a middle-aged Florida shrimp farmer in less

than a decade rise from utter obscurity to the peak of a profession in which he'd had no experience or formal training?

No conventional explanation alone can account for both the breadth and magnitude of Brad's leap and the way he pulled people along in his wake. Something else had to have been in play—some other combination of factors.

One Step at a Time

Like me, like Sara Blakely, and like so many others I interviewed for this book, Brad Margus had no sudden revelation that propelled him into a new life. Even with the advantage of hindsight, he can't point to the single defining break point between then and now. No handy map showed him the way from a Florida shrimp farm to the CEO's office at Perlegen Sciences and to his keynote speech before a Who's Who of genetic research.

Rather, Brad took one step and then another and another, and as he did so, events and circumstances seemed to almost magically arrange themselves around him. He and his wife were alone in their quest, and then they were being carried along on the enthusiasm of others. Brad's focus on his sons' A-T blossomed into something far larger and carried his career with it, and yet Brad never put his livelihood at great risk nor did he ever lose focus on where this all began. By all objective standards, he made the leap from ordinary to extraordinary, but you have to watch the story unfold in super slo-mo to have even a chance of catching the inflection points. And as I was to discover, Brad's story is the rule, not the exception.

A Proper Replacement

"Why me?"

Frances Hesselbein said the same thing back in the spring of 1966 when an acquaintance stopped by to ask if she would consider leading the local Girl Scout troop, which met at the church she attended. They were standing on Frances's creaky wooden front porch in Johnstown, Pennsylvania, a sleepy coal-mining town more famous for the devastating flood that had all but wiped it out 77 years earlier.

Photographs of Frances from that time show her to be an attractive young woman with dark hair and wide-set eyes, almost a Jackie Kennedy look-alike. But her life was decidedly a low-profile one. Married to the editor of the local newspaper and being a mother, she limited her few outside activities to volunteer work at her church. This was the quiet, hometown life Frances had always aspired to, and rather than let it be disrupted, she told the acquaintance she couldn't take on the scout troop.

"I was the mother of a little boy and felt that I didn't know anything about little girls," she remembers. "Then I was again approached, this time with the sad story about how the troop was going to disband because they had lost their leader. I said, 'All right, I'll take them for six weeks, and in the meantime you will find them a proper replacement.'

"So one Monday night I walked into the basement of the Second Presbyterian Church to confront 30 little girls screaming and running around. I told them I was going to be their substitute leader for a while. Years later, the original 30 were in high school, and I was still leading that Girl Scout troop."

Six years after Frances agreed to temporarily take over that first troop, she was invited to lunch with some of the city's most prominent business leaders, including a bank president, the local head of the United Way, and the owner of the Johnstown television station.

"I was acquainted with each of them," Frances says now, "but why lunch with me? Then my lunch companions announced that they had found a new executive director for the regional Girl Scout Council.

"I said, 'Well, that's wonderful. Who is it?'

"And they said, 'It's you!'

"I knew I was not qualified for such an important job, so I turned them down flat. But they wouldn't take no for an answer. 'Well, that's too bad,' they told me, 'because if you don't take it, the Girl Scouts will be thrown out of the United Way.'

"So I said I would do it for six months while they looked for a qualified executive director. I was there for four years."

As hesitant as she was to take the job, Frances was determined to see the work done well. She reinvigorated the local council, assuring that the organization would be able to serve the needs of the region's girls for years to come. In recognition of her excellent work, she was nominated to and served on the Girl Scouts' national and international boards.

Then—almost inevitably, it seems, given the arc of her career—Frances was asked to run the whole show, and she reluctantly (of course) accepted. Fittingly, she arrived in Manhattan to assume her new duties as executive director of Girl Scouts of America on July 4, 1976, the same day the Tall Ships sailed into New York Harbor to celebrate the two-hundredth birthday of the United States.

Frances's tenure saw a remarkable transformation of one of the world's largest and most complex groups—2.25 million girls overseen and supported by 650,000 adult volunteers and paid staff. When she took the national helm, the Girl Scouts were serving mostly white, middle-class communities. Not surprisingly, membership was declining. To broaden the base, Frances committed the Girl Scouts to reaching out to all girls, regardless of race or socioeconomic status. She also replaced a traditional top-down hierarchy with an innovative new structure of shared authority, making the organization more nimble and responsive to the needs of girls and volunteers.

Along the way, Frances gained a worldwide reputation as one of nation's most gifted leaders. Not only did she lecture at Harvard's business school and appear on the cover of *Business Week* magazine; she also became close friends with Peter Drucker, the father of modern management theory. So impressed was Drucker with Frances's accomplishments that, when she retired from the Girl Scouts' national office in 1990, he asked her to head up his Foundation for Nonprofit Leadership, now known as the Leader to Leader Institute.

Today, this stylishly dressed woman with dark, carefully coiffed hair travels the world, speaking about leadership and inspiring new generations to serve. In recognition of her achievements, she has been awarded the Presidential Medal of Freedom, the United States' highest civilian honor.

Could any of this have been predicted more than four decades earlier when Frances was first approached to head up the Johnstown troop? It's hard to see how. Frances was, by her own reckoning, a perfectly content small-town Pennsylvania homemaker. She had accepted her status quo, but she didn't feel as if she was stuck in a rut or that life was passing her by, nor was she propelled by personal tragedy. Frances never sought out the positions that served her as steppingstones to success. In fact, she initially refused nearly all of them. She had no training in leadership, no professional background whatsoever.

Frances, in short, never aspired to be extraordinary. Yet, like Brad Margus, that's precisely what she became—one very slow and reluctant step at a time. And the Girl Scouts of America and the nation as a whole are the better for it.

Breaking from the Past

How is it that some people are able to break from the past and accomplish great things in their lives while others of seemingly equal abilities and resources only get to watch from the sidelines? Why is it that those who do make the break are so often carried on the enthusiasm of others? If you want to make the break yourself, how much do you have to be willing to lay on the table before you try?

Obviously, there is no single answer to those questions. The human experience is too varied for a one-size-fits-all solution. But the paths taken by Sara Blakely, Brad Margus, and Frances Hesselbein do point to a three-part pattern so often repeated by those who have achieved extraordinary lives that it amounts to a virtual physical principle. More important by far, their actions show us all how we can reignite and fulfill our own potential.

Following, then, is an introduction to the three critical steps of a process I refer to as "the leap." I take each of them up at length in the chapters that follow.

1. To Make the Leap, First Find Your Primary Color

You won't believe how liberating it is to be yourself completely.

I use the term Primary Color to describe that one spot on the spectrum where our greatest strengths overlap with our most intense passions. Too many of us never get there. We listen to the myths that keep us stuck in the status quo. We fall victim to the pranks the brain plays on us whenever we try to contemplate a better future for ourselves. But we all have a Primary Color—one that exists for us alone—and living in the light of that color is pure magic.

Think back for a moment to the two people you have just met. Before his sons were diagnosed with A-T, Brad Margus had proven he was good at sales (the shrimp didn't sell themselves) and capable of hard work (the shrimp didn't farm themselves either). But not until those strengths aligned themselves with the deep passion let loose by Jarrett's and Quinn's illness did he truly find his Primary Color and begin down the road that would carry him to the peak of his profession.

Similarly, Frances Hesselbein was always passionate about helping others, but her work with the Girl Scouts, first at the troop level, unveiled a natural talent for leadership that was so obvious to others that Frances was continually summoned to ever more important roles until she was named head of the entire national organization.

Both Brad and Frances found themselves in positions that leveraged their innate strengths and passions every day, both came to live in their Primary Colors, both experienced the tremendous energy that is let loose when strengths and passions are aligned, and both amazed everyone (themselves included) with their performance. But—and this is critical—neither had to change who they were to get there.

The people who knew Brad in college and beyond wouldn't find him much changed today. He's still the same soft-spoken, hard-driving person he has always been. Even now that he's an internationally recognized genetics industry CEO, Brad remains far more prone to polo shirts and jeans than to suits and ties. Sit with him for a while and it's not hard to imagine him back in Florida, tending his shrimp farm.

"I feel like I'm still basically the same guy I was in the shrimp business," Brad told me in his corner office at Perlegen Sciences. "But somehow I feel like I am using much more of myself now."

Frances's journey lacks both the drama and the tragedy of Brad Margus's. She was more pushed by others than pulled by events, but she, too, made the leap from ordinary to extraordinary not by reinventing herself but by letting her latent talent for leadership and a passion for helping others find their natural meeting point. Rather than become someone else, Brad and Frances became more fully themselves.

I can never claim such accomplishments, but the same essential thing happened to me. I knew I was unfulfilled in my job. At some level, I realized I lacked a passion for management consulting and head-hunting, and I certainly hoped that I hadn't maxed out my talents (although at another level I also feared that I had). Most of the time that I was at work, I felt as if I was swimming with sneakers on. The few times I felt truly energized—during the book tour for *5 Patterns*, most notably—I wasn't really doing what I was paid to do, as my boss so astutely observed at our final meeting.

Getting fired freed me of all that, and trying to avoid climbing back on the same treadmill forced me to explore alternative paths. But not until I hit upon the idea of World50 and began to actively promote it did I really understand what it was like to have my passions and skills aligned and fully engaged. Without knowing it, at that moment I also found my Primary Color, and I've been living inside it ever since.

While Frances, Brad, and I stumbled into fulfillment, you can be more methodical. Think of the color wheel you might find in a paint store that allows you to blend colors until you find just the right shade for your living room. That's how it is with careers and life journeys, too. There are three basic "shades" or overlapping areas of competency—leadership, execution, and curiosity—that produce a near-infinite spectrum of possibilities. But each of us has only one *Primary* Color, that single spot where our greatest passions overlap with our greatest strengths.

If your daily activities aren't aligned with that spot, you will never feel totally fulfilled. Find your Primary Color—and in chapter 5, I will give you the specific tools to do that—and the passage from ordinary to extraordinary is less a matter of mastering new skills than a matter of riding the enormous energy released by discovering what you were meant to be all along.

That brings us to the second path.

2. Once You Find Your Primary Color, Bring It to Bear on an Idea That Is Big, Selfless, and Simple

This is how you make certain you don't go it alone.

Again, look back at the brief life stories I've presented so far. In particular, consider the very specific ideas on which we rode into our new lives: SPANX, Sara's creation of a new clothing segment designed by women for women; Brad's quest to advance our understanding and treatment of genetic diseases; Frances's inspiration to embrace diversity within the world's largest organization for girls; and my baby, w50, that brings to life the notion that even the world's most successful executives can benefit from peer support. What are the common elements among these ideas?

It turns out that our successes were derived in no small part from the very nature of the ideas that drove us there. All of us get bombarded every day with hundreds of new ideas, each competing for space on our scarce attention spectrum. Most pass by us like ships in the night, but some—a very few—stick. They grab us, they motivate us to act, and they spread. This is not by coincidence. My research and my own experience show that these ideas share three very distinct characteristics.

First, all the ideas that carried us away from an ordinary life trajectory were *big*. We wanted to crack the code of killer diseases, bring greater diversity to one of the world's biggest organizations for girls, rescue women from the tyranny of uncomfortable and poor-performing undergarments, and liberate the world's top business leaders from the loneliness and isolation of the executive suite. That's a lot of different vehicles, but none of us can be accused of thinking small.

Second, not only were the ideas big, they were also *selfless*. Each of the ideas that propelled us forward and preceded the ultimate leap was focused outward, not inward. Our ambition was for the cause, not for personal accolades. Whether the ideas were directed toward Girl Scouts, women's fashion, high-level executives, or the victims of genetic diseases and their families, they all were first and foremost focused on their beneficiaries, not on those of us who first conceived and pushed them. Had the emphasis been in the opposite direction—toward us rather than away from us—we would have had to trudge forward mostly on our own. Instead, in each case, dozens of other people were drawn to and enlisted in our causes.

The third common thread: all the ideas cited are *simple*. Cutting the feet off panty hose was an inspired concept, but it's not rocket science. Nor was my family of executive networks. In fact, the infrastructure of w50 is surprisingly uncomplicated. That's one of the business's charms. Brad eventually enlisted some of the great scientific minds of our age in his cause, but his original goal—to simply make *some* progress in our understanding of genetic diseases like the one that affected his two sons—was as straightforward as it was compelling. Frances opened up the Girl Scouts and reformed and flattened its moribund leadership structure—no easy task. But her reforms over decades were all in the service of a single, simple goal: increasing the organization's diversity.

Willie Nelson once said that the toughest song to write is the simple song. It's that very simplicity that makes such songs the most compelling. That applies to ideas, too. Simplicity has a tremendous impact on whether an idea takes flight or sits on the tarmac.

Big ideas get noticed; they break through the brain's natural barrier to noise and clutter and get us to pay attention. (Brad Margus's quest to bring the power of genetic research to bear on a rare disease.) Selfless ones appeal to our very deeply seated sense of empathy and create the urge for us to sign on. (Frances Hesselbein's determination to reform and diversity the leadership of the Girl Scouts of America.) Simple ideas spread quickly because they are broadly interpreted and easily translated into action by others. (Sara Blakely's feetless panty-hose.) In concert, big, selfless, and simple ideas attract, inspire, and involve others and create a multiplier effect, resulting in broad achievement beyond what any one person could hope to accomplish alone.

That brings us to the third path, the one that helps us translate big, selfless, and simple ideas into action.

3. Let the Spark Sequence Happen

The Spark Sequence is how you mitigate risk and turn leaps into inevitabilities.

"You gotta know when to hold 'em, know when to fold 'em"—so Kenny Rogers sang in "The Gambler"—"know when to walk away, know when to run." But do you really?

The popular perception, reinforced by tens of thousands of TV and movie hours, is that great success belongs to the most fearless and aggressive in society—people consumed by blind ambition, the ones who dive headfirst into the water without ever checking its depth. However, the people I talked with who made the leap from ordinary to extraordinary didn't come anywhere near fitting that mold.

"I never had the ambition to do any of the things I've accomplished," Frances Hesselbein told me over a cup of tea in her office at the Leader to Leader Institute on Manhattan's Park Avenue. "In fact, for most of my jobs, I didn't knock on a door. I was thrown through a door! But once inside, I realized that was where I was supposed to be."

Brad Margus wasn't thrown through any doors, but he didn't jump blindly either. Impelled forward by his sons' A-T, Brad made a small foray into philanthropy. When that worked, he tried recruiting a scientist to serve on the board of his "temporary" project. And so it went every step of the way until he was CEO of Perlegen. Basically, Brad remained a shrimp farmer with a charitable avocation until years later when the avocation became his calling and his new calling began to define the terms of his life.

Sara Blakely and I fit the same pattern. Neither of us took a spontaneous header out of our old lives into new ones. I didn't have the guts until I knew that the odds of my landing safely on the other side were greater than the odds of my being content with my existing job. Sara, I think, probably did have the courage—that woman got game!—but she had the practical issues of rent and car payments and college loans to deal with. And even Sara stayed with her day job years after her flash of entrepreneurial brilliance and initial success.

Sometimes what stands between an acceptable present and a vibrant future is a combination of position and prestige. A friend of mine, a fellow executive recruiter, had a deep desire to become a full-time writer, but he couldn't bring himself to surrender the cushy pay and perks of his job. So he began writing freelance pieces in his off-hours and submitting them to magazines and newspapers. Just a few pieces were accepted at first, and not all those made it into print. But gradually the momentum built up until editors were calling him and requesting articles. When my friend finally gave up his day job, he was already a full-time writer in his own mind.

In essence, all of us—and you can do it, too—were mitigating downside risk and testing upside potential while we amassed experience equity. Consciously in some cases, unconsciously in others, we were indulging in what I call the Spark Sequence—a series of exploratory events that:

Built exposure to what might lie ahead.

Brad Margus, for example, inched incrementally toward Perlegen. First, he became acquainted with raising money for research. Then, he branched into the research community. Finally, as CEO, he became the one responsible for creating vital links between money, research, and the marketplace.

Created confidence in the skills to get us there and the passion to sustain ourselves once we arrived.

At one level, Frances Hesselbein's pattern of resistance, capitulation, and acceptance could be seen as nothing more than indecision writ large. But without realizing what she was doing, Frances used these intersections of passion, strength, and challenge to slowly bring forth latent skills and talents that had been underutilized, and her success at each new level prepared her for the next repetition of the cycle.

Allowed us to visit our new lives without quite going there.

Witness my pal, the onetime executive recruiter who couldn't resist the lure of a blank page. Once he actually called himself a professional writer, it was, in Yogi Berra's famous words, "like déjà vu all over again."

We all sparked, often multiple times. We felt the pull of a new life and—just as our brains have taught us to do—we resisted it. Rare is the person who can walk out the door and leave it all behind without a single regret. In our guts and our heads and our blood, we understood risk and respected our aversion to it.

We moved to combustion only when our journeys of self-discovery left us no other choice—when the scales were tipped, the seesaw started heading down the other way, the fuse was lit and all desire was gone to stamp it out.

None of us drove risk clear out of the equation. You can't do that when you are making changes of these magnitudes. But through our "sparking," we reduced risk to an acceptable psychological level for each of us.

We leapt not when the chasm between where we were and where we hoped to go was most wide and the danger greatest (that's the great myth of the leap) but when sparking had reduced the chasm to a small fissure and the danger of staying where we were was greater than the danger of moving on. That's the reality I saw time and again in my research, my interviews, and my own life.

THOSE WHO MAKE THE LEAP...

MYTH	REALITY
Reinvent themselves	Become more completely themselves
Charge forward alone	Are carried to success on the shoulders of others
Are daring risk takers	Are keen risk mitigators

From Ordinary to Extraordinary

The leap is not cookie-cutter predictable. It comes at different people from different directions. Sometimes the leap is idea driven—an overwhelming inspiration like Sara Blakely's that arises out of the most mundane circumstances. Sometimes, it's a radical shift in our own history. Personal tragedy kick-started Brad Margus toward his leap. Getting laid off got me off the dime. And as we've just seen, Frances Hesselbein practically had to be pushed uphill into what has become a life of extraordinary accomplishment.

Some of us rushed toward the precipice; some of us crept. Some of us proceeded logically, step by step; some relied more on intuition. Everyone has a different stomach for risk. No two people reason exactly alike. That's one of the beauties of our humanness: our infinite variability.

But however the leap happens, the same three forces are in play. To make the passage from ordinary to extraordinary, Frances, Sara, Brad, and the others profiled in this book first aligned their pursuits with the overlap of their truest passions and their greatest strengths, and thus found their Primary Color.

They then brought their Primary Color to bear on ideas that were big, selfless, and simple, and that ultimately engaged others in their quest: to start a clothing business that would empower women around the world, to inspire a brighter, inclusive future for an encrusted scouting organization—the list goes on.

The alignment of strengths and passions gave them energy and purpose they had never known before. Their big, selfless, and simple ideas gave them wings to fly on. And the Spark Sequence allowed them time to test out their futures until the risks of great change had been mitigated sufficiently and the upside clearly enough defined to permit combustion to happen. With that, the theoretical became real.

Those, in a nutshell, are the three paths at work. From here, we dive deeper into each of the three elements of the leap pattern, all in a quest to answer two simple questions that speak to our deepest longing for purpose as business people, homemakers, professionals, educators, and public servants: Why is it that some people can break free from their existing trajectories in life and accomplish unexpected and incredible things, while most don't? And what can I do, right now, to start and nurture a leap of my own?

My Leap Journal—
The Three Rules

Do I have a deep understanding of my greatest strengths and passions? Are my strengths and passions leveraged at work every day?

Have I been able to enlist others in my work and life dreams? If so, spend some time dissecting why and how. What was it about the work or dream that brought others on board?

How often do I "spark" in new directions?

Primary Colors: Tapping the Energy Within

4

For more than ten years, Stephen Rhinesmith served as the Chief Executive Officer for the American Field Service (AFS), the world's largest international student-exchange program. Created as a nonprofit by the World Congress, AFS each year sends thousands of high school kids from the United States to one of more than 50 host countries around the world. In preparation for their trips, the students gather in New York, where Stephen would stand at a podium and address the excited group.

Deep-voiced and bearded, Stephen said that he must have given essentially the same talk to nearly 100,000 kids during his tenure as head of AFS.

"I would tell them that going overseas and trying something completely new has a great advantage. No one over there knows who you are, so you can be whoever you want to be. But," he says he would add, "this also comes with a great dilemma. You must first answer an essential question: who do you really *want* to be?"

Turns out, high school students aren't the only ones who have a difficult time answering this question.

Treading Water

It's late February 2000, and Jeff Gray is sitting at his desk in Atlanta, slogging through the piles of work in front of him. To the outside world, Jeff has surrounded himself with all the usual trappings of success: a stable job with a visible career path, good pay, a nice house, wife, and kids. But inside, he has begun to have doubts about where all this is leading him.

Jeff began his career on the West Coast, working in an entry-level job in the mortgage banking industry. In the course of his work, he noticed numerous holes that seemed to exist in the system for processing mortgages, so he and a friend started brainstorming how to create a small company that could plug the gaps. Jeff wasn't expecting to hit a home run, but he did believe that with only a few employees, he could generate clients and provide a service, and working for himself seemed much more appealing than working for a large company. He set out on his own and launched Priority Value Check.

Within a few years, the business was providing a range of services for the industry: credit checks, appraisals, and so on. Jeff and his team had found a way to write some very basic software that allowed for the automation of several of these processes—a departure from their original business plan, but this seemed to give the company an opportunity to scale up—until, that is, Microsoft played leapfrog yet again.

Windows 95B was released in the late nineties, just as Priority Value Check was beginning to settle in for the long run, and to Jeff's complete surprise, its significant changes were not compatible with the software Jeff's company had created.

"I guess Bill Gates had different plans for us," Jeff says. "It blew up all our desktop software, and our years of investment in the technology was worthless overnight." (Jeff now uses a Mac.)

Jeff could see that the only way for his small company to survive was to put all its applications online, but he and his partners lacked access to the substantial amount of money required to make the switch. Faced with a dwindling set of options, he put his company on the block, eventually selling it to a start-up technology outfit, RealEstate.com, that seemed willing to make the necessary investment.

Again, "seemed" is the critical word. No sooner had Jeff and his wife, Ellie, moved their family to Atlanta to work with RealEstate.com than the Internet bubble burst, the company declared bankruptcy, and its founder found himself dogged by whispers of fraud and embezzlement.

Jobless in an ever-tightening job market, Jeff turned to providing consulting services on a part-time basis. Fortunately, his clientele quickly grew, and his part-time gig turned into full-time employment. He was in this position when, in February 2000, the doubts began to well up inside him.

"I was actually doing surprisingly well as a consultant, and we were starting to like Atlanta. But looking back, I can see that consulting was a hollow experience for me. It paid well, but basically, I was just treading water."

Finding Refuge

Through their children's school, Jeff and Ellie met Bruce Deel, a self-effacing Atlanta pastor who runs an outreach program called City of Refuge, which serves southwest Atlanta, one of the city's poorest and most crime-ridden neighborhoods. Like many similar urban missions, City of Refuge provides meals, shelter, and other basic services to the homeless.

The Grays had been casually looking for a church to join but hadn't felt comfortable at the establishment churches in their upscale Buckhead neighborhood, so one Sunday the family dropped in on a service at Deel's midtown mission to have a look.

From the moment they walked in the door, Jeff and Ellie felt a powerful connection. "I loved it right off the bat," he says. "The style was raw, not polished. Everyone was in jeans and T-shirts. Homeless people were scattered among other folks from all walks of life. I remember thinking, almost immediately, There are people here, sitting right next to me, who could use my help. I felt compelled to do *something*.

"That day, I volunteered to help cook breakfast every other Saturday for the kids who came over for this program.

"It wasn't anything groundbreaking. There are programs like this all over the place, but it really sucked me in. These people had so many issues going in their lives, and slowly my involvement just grew and grew. Before I knew it, I was doing quite a lot of stuff."

Jeff was primed for such an experience. His wife had survived a completely unexpected and dire cancer diagnosis. And it's not uncommon in such circumstances to want to repay

God for intervening. But that wasn't what motivated him, he says.

"It wasn't a faith-based lightning bolt. I was just blown away by the whole thing. I was amazed that people were living in such horrible situations and that other people would risk going under a freeway bridge at 9 P.M. to hang out with these drug addicts and offer them a sandwich and chance to get off the streets. Getting involved initially might have appealed more to my sense of adventure than anything else if I was being totally candid. But it wasn't just curiosity—I was deeply moved. This was not some feel-good charity fund-raiser. These were real people with desperate, urgent needs.

"Then the idea hit me all at once that people were walking right by these awful problems. All of us out in the suburban world are so insulated from anyone who doesn't look, smell, talk, or sound exactly like us. I can't put a date or time to that, but this is the gut feeling that really started to motivate me.

"I kept thinking that somebody at some point has to be willing to help, because no one seemed to be jumping in. And at City of Refuge you were really needed. If someone didn't show up on a Saturday, the meals didn't get served."

Jeff's motivation spurred him to be even more active. He got involved with inmates at the Fulton County jail and with the county court system. At one point, he, Ellie, and their children even took a woman from the City of Refuge shelter into their home for six months.

"Don't Ask"

Jeff continued with his day job—he had to—but as his night-and-weekend job expanded, spare time dropped out of the picture. "I'd leave a meeting, peel off my suit and tie, run home, talk to Ellie and the kids for a little while, then head out under a bridge somewhere."

One night at around 11:00 Jeff was hard at work in his home office, preparing some documents that he was to present the next day at a vital meeting in San Francisco, when his cell phone rang. Wailing on the other end of the line was Al, a homeless drug addict Jeff had come to know through his City of Refuge work. Al owed money to a drug dealer who had come after him with a two-by-four, smashing both his legs. In tears and straining to speak, Al told Jeff that unless he could come up with another $24, the dealer had even more dire plans for him.

"There I was, sitting at my computer in my warm, secure home in Buckhead, the kids fed and tucked neatly in bed, and I was thinking, 'Now what in the world do I do with this?!'" Jeff recalls. "I thought back to a personal promise I had made that I would not walk by these situations, but this was a big challenge. I was completely unsure of myself. I instinctively began putting on a pair of jeans and T-shirt when Ellie said, 'Where are you going?' I looked at her and sighed, 'Don't ask.'"

Jeff jumped in his car and started to head in Al's direction. "My breath was quickening. I called up this buddy who ran our shelter, picked him up, and together we drove in silence into a part of town that was then entirely unfamiliar to me. My eyelids felt stapled open, as if I was passing through the giant doors of Jurassic Park. I was scared to death." The streets were dark, lined mostly with abandoned buildings. People were walking about aimlessly or just sleeping on the sidewalk.

Leaning nervously over the dashboard, the two men approached what Jeff thought might be the spot where Al was waiting. Jeff's cell phone suddenly broke the silence.

"The phone flew out of my hand! I picked it up again. It was Al calling back.

"'Where are you?' I barked anxiously.

"'I'm down on the corner. Come quick!'

"I told Al to stand up as best he could so we could see him. Then I stomped on the gas and raced down the street. We stopped just long enough to throw him in the backseat and tore off again. We must have gone almost 20 blocks before anyone said anything."

With the adrenaline rush beginning to subside, the reality of the situation started to sink in. "It was midnight and Al's knees were in pretty bad shape. I took him over to Grady Memorial Hospital so they could take a look while I waited. At about 4 A.M. he was released, so I dropped him off at the shelter and got back home at 5:00. Then I had to make a 7:30 plane."

With his project not yet completed, Jeff worked on his computer the entire flight.

"In the blink of an eye, I'm in this boardroom on the other side of the country, negotiating a very significant and complicated deal, and I'm thinking to myself, 'This is so surreal. If these guys knew where I had been just a few hours ago, they wouldn't think I was stable enough to do business with!'"

"My Entire Definition of Success Has Changed"

As insane as it sounds, this was basically Jeff's life for the first three years after he walked into Bruce Deel's unassuming church. Not all the events were so dramatic—they couldn't be!—but cognitive dissonance between where he had been and where he was headed was ever present.

"I had to balance all this," he says. "It was really hard." Then his tipping point finally occurred.

"I ended up with an office at the church. I was there more than anyone else. I remember looking up at my colleague Ruth one day and saying, 'Hey, I think I work here now.' Right at that time, my only remaining consulting client told me, 'Listen, we really like you as a person, but you're not really doing much for us. Why don't you finish up this last piece of the contract, and then do the shelter thing full time. We're not firing you, but you really need to pick what you want to do. We've discussed it and concluded that you aren't going to pick us.' They were right."

Jeff, in fact, had found his Primary Color at the intersection of his passion to help the dispossessed and troubled of Atlanta and his natural talent for entrepreneurship—for jumping in and getting things done. Now, he started to truly live inside his Primary Color's light.

For a time he became a paid employee of the City of Refuge. On the side, to support the growing financial needs of his family, Jeff nursed along a small catering company that he had launched a few years earlier. Almost inevitably, the seemingly independent threads of his new life began slowly to converge.

Jeff introduced catering at the mission as one track to help bring the homeless back into the workforce. Not only did his catering company give employment to dozens of rehabilitated homeless people, it also introduced these inspirational people to Jeff's clients, who were mostly upper-income suburbanites hosting dinner parties. One event at a time, Jeff began building significant support for his work.

When I interviewed Jeff, he was only a month away from opening what he has labeled, with great entrepreneurial flair, the City of Refuge's 180-Degree Kitchen, a restaurant staffed almost entirely by successful graduates of the City of Refuge's own programs.

"The restaurant will handle all our feeding, 8,000 meals a month, but it's also the center of a culinary-arts program for sixteen-to-twenty-five-year-old inner-city kids," Jeff almost gushed. "It took us a couple of years and a couple of million dollars to build, and that money was hard to raise. But what's exciting is that I'm taking over all that responsibility now. We will cater to corporations and individuals all over Atlanta, but more important, we can turn out several hundred graduates a year who will have a brighter future."

Asked what his work with the Kitchen and with City of Refuge has ultimately meant to him, Jeff first quoted Ralph Waldo Emerson: "Every man has his own vocation. Talent is the call. There is one direction in which all space is open to him. . . . He is like a ship in a river; he runs against obstructions on every side but one; on that side all obstruction is taken away and he sweeps serenely over a deepening channel into an infinite sea."

Then he grew more personally reflective: "You know, making the money work has been extremely difficult, but life is lived to the full. On sunny days I walk around all those shiny downtown glass office buildings, look up to the top corner offices that I used to covet, and wonder what exactly they are thinking. I am sure that path is right for some, but I do wonder, is it right for everyone in that building? My entire definition of success has changed.

"I finally found this place where I was most effective. It feels like I am where I'm supposed to be and that I'm doing what I am supposed to be doing—that I'm being moved by a force greater than myself.

"That's what the Emerson quote says to me: when you line up with what you are good at and maybe what you are called to do, the obstructions all just fade away."

Such is the power of living in the light of your Primary Color.

From Fixing Weaknesses to Focusing on Strengths

Who do you want to be?

And how do you know when you arrive?

As I wrote earlier, there's no single answer to either question. Indeed, until you find your Primary Color, the questions are almost unintelligible. Once you do find it, though, the issues of who you want to be and how you know you've become that person all but answer themselves. The transformative effect is simply too great to be ignored.

As we've just seen, Jeff Gray was on a traditional career path with all the usual ups and downs until he arrived at a new definition of success. Rather than measure himself by salary and material possessions, he began measuring himself by his impact on the neediest immediately around him. And as that happened, he stopped swimming against the current of his essential self.

Like most of us in the workplace, Jeff had spent the bulk of his time fixing his weaknesses. Now, he found himself focusing on his strengths. He pitched in and did what he could see needed to be done, and what he had time to do, given his day job—and, so subtly that he didn't at first know what was happening, his priorities shifted, obstacles faded away, and unplanned horizons opened up.

What had begun as acts of volunteerism turned into leadership positions. Jeff opened new programs. He tied his catering business to the mission's work-training program. The new momentum of his life pulled the catering and work-training programs together, and the 180-Degree Kitchen was born.

When you find your Primary Color, life unfolds in marvelous, unplanned, and unplannable ways. In Jeff's case, all this was accompanied by the kinds of heroics that are the stuff of prime-time TV: rescuing addicts one moment, hopping on planes the next to close business deals on the other side of the continent.

Jeff would not argue that he was a natural genius. No one profiled in this book would come anywhere near saying that. But by finding our Primary Colors, all of us opened ourselves up to the best that was within us, and that is about as close to genius as anyone ever gets. When talent, passion, and commitment are in harmony, horizons are unveiled. You see, almost literally, opportunity where before you saw stone walls. As happened with Jeff, and with Brad Margus, Frances Hesselbein, and Sara Blakely, roads converge and lead off into still more directions.

In fact, the leap is filled with force multipliers like that. Finding your Primary Color does more than align passions and strengths. It also aligns your efforts and even your career trajectory with your own best interests. Because you are doing what you like and are good at, you strive to get better; and because you strive to get better, you do exactly that. It's not DNA that makes perfect; it's practice and the motivation to do so.

When Work Becomes Play

Today, the idea that practice makes perfect is so accepted it's a cliché, but four centuries ago, it would have bordered on intellectual heresy.

In 1546, over a dinner in Rome, Alessandro Cardinal Farnese asked the painter and architect Giorgio Vasari to assemble a catalogue of artists and their works. Four years later, Vasari published in Florence the first edition of *The Lives of the Most Eminent Painters, Sculptors, and Architects*—a deeply influential work still much consulted by art historians.

Among other firsts, Vasari coined the term "Renaissance," or its Italian equivalent, *Rinascimento.* But in some ways, his insistence that artistic genius is innate, not learned, had the more enduring effect. To achieve true greatness, you pretty much had to be blessed at birth. Once blessed, success was more a matter of letting nature's gifts flow through you than of cultivating and improving those gifts through diligent practice. As Vasari once wrote, "Men of genius sometimes accomplish most when they work the least, for they are thinking out inventions and forming in their minds the perfect idea that they subsequently express with their hands."

Recent studies, however, have shown that Vasari was at least partially wrong, and maybe entirely so. Scientific experts are producing remarkably consistent findings from a broad range of fields. Rather than being innate, great talent appears to be largely the result of exactly what finding your Primary Color leads you to: great motivation and the focused practice that follows as a matter of course.

Tiger Woods wasn't born with a sand wedge in his hands, but at his father's urging, he first swung a golf club at age eighteen months and to this day has never stopped trying to improve. Nor were Warren Buffett or other highly successful investors born with a Midas touch. Buffett famously spends untold hours poring over the financial reports of the companies he and Berkshire Hathaway are considering for investment—or divestment.

And so it is with most people who achieve the highest levels of performance. They get there not via their genes but through endless hours of practice, and not just any practice. The real difference, so researchers are learning, is what's known as "deliberate practice"—that is, practice that requires focus and full mental engagement, is specifically intended to improve performance, reaches for objectives beyond one's level of competence, and provides feedback on results.

By its very nature, deliberate practice cannot be measured by the raw accumulation of hours. That's what assembly-line workers do and indeed what so much of paid labor at all levels is about: putting in time, going through the motions. Deliberate practice is about time plus the passion that enriches the time and makes the clock disappear.

Deliberate practice cannot be externally imposed nor the motivation behind it bought or bribed out of someone. In fact, a vast body of research literature going back over many decades suggests just the opposite. We do best at what we want to do, worst at what we are forced to do.

In one frequently cited study from the mid-1980s, Brandeis University psychology professor Teresa Amabile had 72 creative-writing students compose and submit poetry. Before they were sent off to complete the assignment, one group was encouraged to think of the tangible rewards of their work—possible fellowships, the impression on their teachers, publication, etc. Another group got a pep talk on the internal rewards of poetry composition—the joy of playing with words, of finding the right meter and rhythm for the subject. A third group received the assignment but with no attempt to influence how they approached it. The resulting poems were then submitted to a dozen poets for judging.

The results? Group A, the ones motivated by external rewards, were judged collectively to be poorer poets by a wide margin. Group C, those given no preamble, finished in the middle; and Group B, those encouraged to draw inspiration from within, walked away with the title.

Other studies have produced similar results. Kindergarten-age artists who are paid on a quantitative basis for the drawings they turn out—with candy, other treats, or some special activity—paint less frequently than contemporaries who draw for the fun of it. Teens who are paid actual cash to perform intellectual tasks show neither the skill nor the enthusiasm of teens presented with the same tasks for no reward.

Of course, money matters, especially to those who have the least of it. But study after study shows that the motivational effect of money diminishes rapidly for individuals once annual earnings cross roughly the poverty line and diminishes equally for societies once the gross domestic product per person exceeds about $8,000.

The University of Rochester's Edward Deci showed almost

four decades ago that people who see themselves as working solely for money or the approval of others or in direct competition against their coworkers take less pleasure in the tasks and perform more poorly on them than those who are internally motivated. There's no real surprise in that. Work yields the greatest performance when it is most like play, and it is most like play when you do it because you want to—that is, when you do it because your strengths and passions are both compelling you in that direction. That's when you learn the most and the fastest. That's when you stop watching the clock and quit comparing yourself to others—when you begin measuring your progress and even your success not by someone else's scale but by your internal standards.

When that happens, the journey takes over, because by then it has become your journey alone, toward a destination that is waiting for no one other than you to arrive. That's what the City of Refuge was for Jeff Gray, the Girl Scouts for Frances Hesselbein, World50 for me. Every destination is different, but once you start the journey toward it, the energy that is released within you is absolutely amazing.

Energy Makers and Breakers

I love this little test of whether you are an introvert or an extrovert: When you go to a party and are around other people, do you gain energy or do you lose it? Extroverts gain it. They're magnetic. They suck up energy from those around them. Meanwhile, introverts lose it. They're the ones giving their energy so the extroverts can have more.

The same is true with Primary Colors. The energy that

accompanies and grows from full engagement is the most important resource in the workplace—far more important than time. And unlike time, energy is expandable. Working in a job that leverages your Primary Color feeds your energy reserves. Working in a job that requires you to constantly correct your weaknesses in the pursuit of a goal you are not passionate about sucks your energy away. One makes you an extrovert in ways that go far beyond social skills; the other renders you an introvert in more settings than just looking at your shoes while you try to talk with someone.

Locating your Primary Color—finding the exact point of intersection of your strengths and weaknesses—puts your brain on overdrive. It opens up possibilities that have always been there for you but that also have long been hidden. In the light of your Primary Color, the future moves toward you as the status quo recedes into the background.

However, living in your Primary Color also has three specific neural effects that serve as force multipliers. They are outlined here.

Engagement with your Primary Color in the workplace increases focus and attention, and focused attention stabilizes and expands the brain's circuitry.

One of the themes that emerged time and again in my conversations with people who had made the leap was how simple the everyday tasks of work became. Turns out, there's a good reason for that. Aligning your central talent and passion inevitably increases the attention you pay to your work, and attention is, in a sense, its own reward.

In a 2005 article for the United Kingdom's *Philosophical Transactions of the Royal Society of London,* physicist Henry Stapp and psychiatrist Jeffrey Schwartz showed that sustained concentrated attention on any particular mental experience—a thought, an insight, an image, even a fear—not only kept the brain circuitry involved open and alive but also eventually produced physical changes in the brain's structure. In effect, by increasing attention, you are creating brain architecture specifically suited to the challenges before you. Little wonder, then, that performance should grow dramatically.

Engagement with your Primary Color also increases your own expectations of success, and expectations drive reality.

The placebo effect is well established: tell a patient a pill will relieve his or her pain, and it's likely to do that even if all you give the patient is sugar compressed into tablet form. Studies have shown that placebo pain pills can be nearly as effective as aspirin—and even relatively low doses of morphine—in not just easing the expectation of pain but in producing actual systemic changes in the pain centers of the brain. Expectations, in short, can and do drive reality.

So it is, too, with your Primary Color. When talent and passion are in unison, when you *know* you are doing what you were meant to do, the expectation of success increases, confidence rises, and all the built-in signals of the brain that warn us against change and try to steer us toward the status quo begin to dim. Success isn't assured, but a predisposition toward being successful alters both the brain's chemistry and its structure.

Inspirations and insights become more common. Linkages open up between parts of the brain that have rarely been in communication. We're more creative because the brain keeps rewarding us for our creativity, and the greater rewards make us more productive still, and not only in our specific field of practice.

K. Anders Ericsson of Florida State University, one of the leading proponents of "deliberate practice" and other researchers have found, for example, that doctors who improve their diagnostic performance on specific cases through deliberate practice also improve their capacity to come up with accurate diagnoses on cases outside their immediate expertise. Not only do specific areas of the brain benefit from this fusion of passion and strength, but the entire spectrum of cognitive abilities seems to be enriched.

There's a spillover effect in another, related way as well. Just as the expectations within our brains create their own reality—the placebo effect—so the expectation of success that comes with finding and living inside our Primary Colors creates a reality of its own. The passion leads to deliberate practice; the practice strengthens talents; and the combination of passionate involvement and strengthened talents yields an energy flow that becomes the harbinger of ultimate success.

Virtually every study I have seen lately of workplace stress and lack of productivity cites the same rough list of reasons. Employees are given too much or too little to do. There's a pervasive uncertainty about what's expected and how performance will be judged. Square pegs are forever being crammed into round holes and reviewed on how well they fit. In the short term, frequent and random interruptions prevent adequate attention to necessary tasks, while in the long term, career ambiguity destroys focus and creates a fundamental paradox:

how do you get better at what you're not sure you want to be? And no one, it seems, feels in control—of the workday, the work space, the work itself, or the work future.

Finding your Primary Color is the way out of that bind. When you are truly engaged in what you are doing, when you've found your Primary Color and are working within its light, you experience the same cascading effect that Jeff Gray and all the others you have already met in these pages experienced. Talent and passion feed off and strengthen one another. Performance swells. Satisfaction, quite simply, goes off the charts.

What Do You Want to Be?

How to find your own specific Primary Color and begin down the path that will lead to your leap and a more fulfilled life is the subject of the chapter that follows. It includes a framework that will help point you in the right direction and a link to a Web site and a self-test I have established to help you discover your Primary Color and interpret the results.

Before we get there, though, ask yourself this one question: what work would you do if you had no restraints—if you could be whatever you wanted to be and absolutely no one knew anything about you or your past history?

If, after serious consideration, the answer to the question "What do you want to be?" is "Exactly what I'm doing now," skip to chapter 6. You have already found your Primary Color. Otherwise, I urge you to read on here. The journey of self-discovery is about to begin.

My Leap Journal—Primary Colors: Tapping the Energy Within

When do I feel most alive at work? Outside work?

What talents or skills have I mastered? What would others say I am exceptionally good at?

What talents or skills am I not able to use?

What do I want to learn?

What am I most passionate about?

What do I like to practice?

For what things do I enjoy the challenge of working to get better?

What things should I stop doing right now?

What are my underdeveloped, underutilized resources?

When do I feel fully alive?

What activities make me feel that life is worth living?

What Is My Primary Color?   **5**

When my first book, *5 Patterns*, was published and began to draw favorable reviews, one of the nation's largest outplacement firms contacted me about using the book to help counsel the displaced executives who made up the bulk of the firm's clientele. I was naturally flattered, and since I had just been fired from my job—a fact I didn't readily divulge—I jumped at the firm's suggestion that I take a free tour through all its testing and counseling services. And thus began one of the more arduous experiences of my life.

In all, I must have answered easily a thousand questions and gone through a dozen or more different tests, including the Myers-Briggs Type Indicator, the venerable and famous personality inventory with roots that reach back to Carl Jung. At the end, once the last question had been answered, I sat down with the coach who had been assigned to me for evaluation and quickly realized that, while I had learned tons about testing and several surprising things about myself, I had discovered almost nothing useful about the most important question in my life at that point: *where do I take my career?*

One set of questions, for example, compared me to thousands of other managers on something like 30 different attributes. In every case but two, I was ranked between the twenty-fifth and seventy-fifth percentiles. Perhaps I should have been comforted to find myself in the middle of the pack, but it felt more like a confirmation of my maddening averageness. And what was I supposed to do with a ranking like this?

Even Myers-Briggs was a disappointment. The test ultimately groups you into one of 16 personality types based on whether you are more comfortable with extroversion (E) or introversion (I) and more inclined to sensing (S) or intuition (N), thinking (T) or feeling (F), and judging (J) or perceiving (P). You're then assigned a four-letter combination of the eight possible initials, based on your responses, and the initials are supposed to capture your personality. INFPs, for example, are "idealistic, loyal to their values and to people who are important to them; curious; adaptable, flexible, and accepting unless a value is threatened." For most takers of this test, the information is interesting and even in some cases shockingly accurate. But again, what are you supposed to do with it? Where's the "so what," the *aha!* moment?

I can now only vaguely remember what my combination of initials was or what it meant. What I do recall thinking is that, while my wife might find the results revealing, I had only discovered who I supposedly was now but not who I might or should be.

And so it was with the whole battery of tests. They provided me with accurate descriptors of myself, but for the most part they gave me a hazy, convoluted, and largely confusing snapshot of how my current reality might or might not play into a better future. The analysis was dripping with *data*, but the data never coalesced into vectors of any sort—arrows that could drive my story line forward. Thus, while information about me spilled off every page, *actionable* information was rarer than hen's teeth, and that, in the end, was all I was really looking for.

How was it that I had spent so much time in the hands of highly competent professionals, using many of the best tools in the business, and was still left empty-handed when it came to the questions that mattered most to me?

The lessons to be learned from these tests, I finally decided, were twofold.

Keep it simple.

At the most basic level, I had learned so much about myself that the various threads of insight were short-circuiting one another. This is a case—one of many, in fact—in which more information can actually be a disadvantage.

In trying to understand why emergency-room doctors tend to overdiagnose heart attacks in older and overweight people and underdiagnose them in women and younger people, medical researchers came to a similar opinion. The weight or age or sex of the supposed victims kicked off all sorts of tangential assumptions that clouded the reality before the doctors' eyes. The answer: cut down on the variables. Look for two, three, at most four things only. Once you've figured out if the patient in front of you is presenting with a heart attack, *then* move on to whether he or she fits a pattern or not. In fact, statistics show conclusively that using *less* information to diagnose heart attacks in the ER dramatically improves successful diagnostic rates.

Business theorists are discovering the same thing. In his book *The Ultimate Question: Driving Good Profits and True Growth*, Fred Reichheld, director emeritus of the global consulting giant Bain & Co., makes a compelling case that the simpler business metrics are, the easier they are to grasp and translate into useful activity.

Rather than measure customer satisfaction by long, involved surveys that can take up to 30 minutes and more to complete—shades of my hours and days of outplacement testing!—Reichheld advocates reducing the metric to a single "ultimate" question, rated on a one-to-ten scale: "Would you recommend us to a friend?" Scores of six and below (Detractors, Reichheld calls them) are then subtracted from scores of nine and ten (Promoters), and the resulting figure is a business's Net Promoter Score.

Traditional market research firms largely abhor the simplicity of Reichheld's approach, with obvious reason: complicating customer satisfaction is their mother's milk. But Reichheld is adamant in defending his one-number approach.

"I can appreciate those who think that satisfaction is too complex to be explained by a single metric," he told me during a lunch. "But what we have learned is that the more metrics you use to measure loyalty, the more difficult progress becomes.

"It's like driving a car. All the elements on the dashboard are very valuable diagnostics of how the car is operating and what speed you're traveling at, but what you really need is the one-number picture you get by looking out the windshield. That's where the brain is consolidating an accurate picture of where you are headed—and what changes are required."

That's exactly where my hours and hours of testing had left me: swamped with current metrics but with no window into my own future.

Keep it relative.

The fact is the human brain is incredibly and understandably deficient in its ability to look at things in absolute terms and incredibly (and again understandably) efficient in looking at things in relative terms. "This is heavy," for example, has virtually no meaning unless we can answer the question *Relative to what?* Relative to the strength of the person making the statement? (A Charles Atlas, say, or a 99-pound weakling?) Relative to another object that is lighter—like a ton of feathers or a pound of bricks? Or relative to the gravitational field in question—a ton of feathers on Earth vs. a ton of feathers on the moon?

So it is with jobs and callings and career trajectories. They can't be judged or even perceived, at least in any meaningful way, in absolute terms. They have to be seen relatively. The questions to ask aren't What is my personality type? or What are my aptitudes? or What does "IFNP" mean? Rather, we should ask Where do my strengths and passions lie relative to where I am? Does my job or my trajectory overlap with either or both? If not, am I getting closer to or further away from that point? That is, where am I relative to where I should be and where I am going?

That's part of the issue of seeing things in relative terms. The other part is depth perception. Information that arrives linearly, along a single axis—IQ tests, SAT scores, salary compensation per peer group, etc.—tells us where we are on a scale related to however large the test group is. But it doesn't give us any purchase on the numbers or any way to act on them. By contrast, information delivered on an x- *and* y-axis grid offers us perception. It shows us the intersections to reach for and the ones to avoid. And by doing so, it provides us with the most valuable feedback of all: *direction*.

Finding what your strengths are—the subject of much outplacement (and intake) testing—gives you a vital piece of the puzzle, but only one piece. Learning where your passions lie provides another critical piece. But the key is to then translate knowledge about strength and passion into action and direction. Until that link is made, all the rest of the information is just words on paper, meaningless counseling across an empty table.

How Do I Get There from Here?

Imagine for a moment that you are coming to the United States for the first time. Through some amazing stroke of luck, you have been given the opportunity to live anywhere in the country that you want. What's more, you have been provided with a complete Frommer's guide—packed with massive detail about every city—to help you with your search. So, on your flight, you read up on your possible new locations and finally settle on San Diego. It seems nice, the weather is perfect, jobs are plentiful, the ocean is nearby.

Great—you have solved the first part of the equation: where you want to go. But the other and equally critical half remains: how to get there. Maybe San Diego is right down the interstate if you are flying into Los Angeles International. Maybe it's all the way across the country if you're landing in New York or Washington, DC, or Atlanta. But until you can lay your hands on a map of the country and plot the coordinates between your airport and San Diego, you can't possibly know what direction to take. And that is the one thing you won't find in the tidal wave of Frommer's data you have been provided: the map that will show you how to get to where you want to go.

The testing industry is, in fact, packed with Frommer's guides to you. These companies compete with one another on the accuracy with which they can describe you. They give you lots of interesting data, but they lack the essential map. They pique your curiosity with glimpses of what your strengths and preferences might be, but they never show you what to do with the information. The tests tell you San Diego is where you most want to live and then exclude any directions. No wonder so many people end up longing for Southern California while heading along an interstate that leads them straight to Canada. Not until it snows in June do they realize they have been traveling the wrong road all along.

What is really needed is a framework, a set of tools that can speak to the questions most important to us: Is my current position aligned with my strengths and passions? Is my career trajectory carrying me toward or away from the point where I can best realize my potential? Without this, the Now Trap closes in on us and we stay the course, never realizing the direction has been wrong until our back is against the wall and changing is the hardest and most risky. We need, in short, information that compels us to act now, when a course correction is still plausible.

Finding the Data That Matter

The best estimates are that a typical unabridged dictionary catalogues no fewer than 11,000 words to describe human ability. That's not really a surprise. Mankind has always quested for more precise ways to capture and illustrate human behavior and performance, We've tried fact-based research, anecdotes, inductive and deductive reasoning, appeals to faith and superstition, and in the end we've arrived at *11,000 words.*

The number itself is staggering—so staggering, in fact, that it convinces us that ability and performance are beyond comprehension. But we don't need to be so overwhelmed. In reality, ability and performance are much more specifically explainable than we have previously understood, as long as we don't bog ourselves down in complexity. All you need are three or four essential pieces of information. Or in my case, two.

I wrote earlier that my time with the outplacement firm was almost totally useless. Note the word *almost*. In fact, I did learn two things about myself, both of immense value. The first was that, compared to the same peer pool of more than a thousand managers, I ranked in the top .5 percent in my ability to enlist others in a common cause. The other was that, on creativity and innovation, I ranked in the same top .5 percent.

Why were these two items so important when the rest of the results were only so many numbers on a page?

1. They told me my most dramatic points of differentiation from the crowd—my relative *dissimilarities* as opposed to my absolute *similarities*.

2. They represented points of both strength (as measured by the test) and passion (as measured by my heart). And, in fact, I immediately recognized them as a point of intersection where each could vitalize the other.

3. These first two little nuggets of information gave me a goal to shoot for. I had discovered my San Diego. I knew where it was. Now I just needed to find a way there.

Mind you, I still didn't know where I was headed—this was a metaphorical San Diego, not the real one—but from that time forward, I began to subconsciously arrange my endeavors so that they would bring my strengths and passions together.

World50 would still have a leisurely gestation period, but it was conceived at the moment I brought those two items of self-awareness together. Everything else I learned about myself in those hours upon hours of testing was distracting background noise. Those two nuggets of gold cut to the chase.

That's what the testing tool I've developed does: It cuts to the chase. It gets rid of the chatter. It simplifies the hunt and leads you to the relational, dimensional information about yourself that you can truly use to set out on your own new trajectory. And then it takes the essential next step and answers two questions: Where am I relative to my current job? and Where is my career headed if I stay on my current path?

These are actionable questions—life-changers—and it is imperative that we address them head-on.

I had to find that direction on my own, stumbling through trial and error, which is why my ride to World50 was not always glassy smooth. You don't have to do that. I can't guarantee that there won't be bumps along the way for you as well, but I *can* guarantee that the testing tool that follows will certainly get you asking the right questions and put the right road map in your hands.

The Roots of Human Ability

Just about all human activity has a bias toward complexity because that's where the intermediaries—the hedge-fund managers, medical diagnosticians, psychiatrists, or, for that matter, outplacement firms—rake in the money. But, in fact, the roots of human ability are fairly simple. They boil down to three basic competencies:

- Curiosity—the inclination to question, to seek information, to understand what has been learned, to grasp what is truly real. This is the search for truth.
- Leadership—the ability to inspire, to move forward, to forge new ground and bring others along. Its many forms include character in the face of adversity, originality, and also beauty and attraction. This is the ability to define direction and draw others toward it.
- Execution—the ability to carry out a task, to get things done, to see a project to conclusion once pointed in the right direction. This also includes the willingness to try, to step up, to dive in.

These three competencies exist in different intensities in all of us. They overlap to form *creativity*, *management*, *innovation*, *reengineering*, and literally every other competency imaginable, in the same way the primary colors of the spectrum—red, blue, and green—overlap to create every other color we know of.

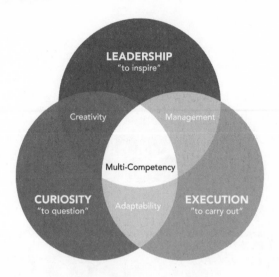

3 COMPETENCIES

There are three Primary Competencies—Leadership, Curiosity and Execution—which overlap to create secondary competencies and all other forms of human performance. Together, they make up a spectrum of ability within which we can discover our own unique Primary Color and assess it against our current job and future career path. (Flip over the book jacket to see this image in color.)

But the point is (a) it all begins with *curiosity*, *leadership*, and *execution*, and (b) every single one of us has her own unique mix of those fundamental three qualities—a competency print that's as singular as a finger- or retina print.

It's when you are forced to work within someone else's definition of your strengths that you become the introvert I wrote about in the last chapter—the one who gives up energy to everyone around him. Exactly the opposite is the case when

STRENGTHS AND PASSIONS SPECTRUM

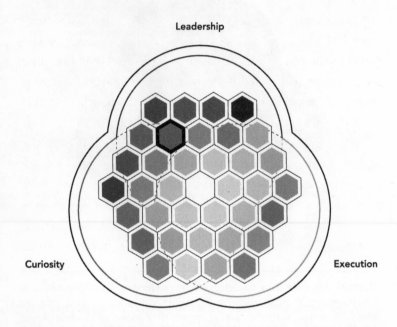

Everyone has a point on the spectrum where our greatest strengths align with our truest passions. (Flip over the book jacket to see this image in color.)

the competencies required of you by your job and your career align with your unique competency print. Then you are the one gathering energy everywhere you go.

Some of us travel figuratively thousands of miles before we get to the point of alignment; others walk through an open door and find that critical intersection waiting there, as Jeff Gray did when he walked into the City of Refuge mission. Some merely tweak their lives while others redefine them entirely. Andy Levine is one of those who had almost no distance to go to discover a new life trajectory.

For years, Andy had thought of himself as the proverbial "sixth man."

"I was only moderately athletic, and it seemed the only times I would excel was when I was willing to work harder than anyone else. I was talented in basketball but not quite good enough to be one of the starting five players," he says. "Instead, I was the first guy to come off the bench—the one they call the 'sixth man,'—and I was valued for it."

In college, Andy kept up the pattern of being just on the edge of breaking through. "I was asked to join my fraternity's band because I could book gigs for us. I am not sure they even plugged my guitar in most nights." Andy knew it was unrealistic to think that he could make a career out of performing, so instead he started to pitch in and help other bands. Then he followed that path to become a band manager.

Several of the bands he worked with eventually took off, including Creed and Sister Hazel, but Andy struggled personally in his role. Rock music can be a cutthroat industry, and Andy learned early on that a person's word in the business was not always his bond. Almost as bad were the endless squabbles with venue managers and record labels over bookings, release dates, tour schedules, and the like. In time, his enthusiasm went south. What had once been a dream job was now just work, and he could see that someday it would turn to drudgery.

Andy knew what his passion was: he loved rock and the joyous release that comes when great music is being played in front of an appreciative audience. He felt certain he had the managerial and promotional strengths and the entrepreneurial skills to make music his life's work even if he couldn't play for a living. But in his role as a band manager, his passion and strengths were pulling against each other and draining the life out of each. Then, in a relative instant, Andy found a way to make them work in unison.

A national alternative-rock and adult-pop station, 99X, that had sprung up in the mid-1990s was, on paper, a huge hit. Ratings were sky-high for the prototype broadcaster, but sell-through was miserable. The station had plenty of listeners and lots of ads, at least initially. According to the demographics, the listeners also had plenty of money—they seemed to be mostly soccer moms—but they weren't buying what the advertisers were selling, probably because they were too busy schlepping their kids to games and school and birthday parties.

That was one side of the equation. On the other side were all the alternative and adult-pop bands that Andy had managed and made contact with over his years in the business. Almost to a group, they wanted to connect in a more personal way with their fan base, but other than frenzied club and stadium dates and the grind of touring, the bands had no venue for doing so.

In textbook economics, this represents a classic opportunity: huge demand, as shown by the radio station's ratings, but no product, as evidenced by the lack of a channel through which bands could engage their fans. Andy's *aha!* moment led to the creation of a venue where fans and bands could come together for a celebration of the music itself.

"For the band Sister Hazel we had mobilized hundreds of fans as a 'street team' to help call radio stations, put up fliers, etc. They had really put in a lot of work and in return demanded that they get to spend some time with the band. I came up with the idea for a cruise, sent out an e-mail, and within two weeks had 400 people signed up."

The Sister Hazel experience was so successful that Andy quickly went on to launch "Rock Boat," the highly successful floating music festivals that are projected to earn his company (aptly named Sixthman) $15 million in sales in only its fifth year.

To find his Primary Color, Andy had only to align his existing strengths and passions with an opportunity that was waiting to be exploited. He turned the corner, the chance was waiting there, and he grasped the possibilities that presented themselves. Some take a different route, even stepping back into their own past to find the point where competencies aligned and their Primary Color shone the brightest.

Back to the Future

After college, Richard Singer spent two years in the Peace Corps in Burkina Faso, teaching African villagers on the edge of the Sahara how to dig wells. He knew the work was temporary, a way station on the path to full adulthood, and when his tour was over and he returned to the States, Richard set out to join the rest of the worker ants on their march toward material success. Eventually he would earn an MBA and go on to a succession of jobs that finally led to a position as controller at an internationally recognized art museum in Washington, DC.

Richard was married to a lawyer. They had a house in northwest DC, a live-in nanny for their daughter, enough money for the right restaurants, and enough standing that he could join the right club at which to play squash, which he had taken up in college. Thanks to his job, he also had entrée to some of the splashiest art exhibit openings in the nation's capital.

On paper, he was living the American Dream. He had worked hard in school and now had a stable job with a good dose of pay and prestige. The only problem was the same one faced by so many of us: Richard's work brought him little satisfaction. He could do the job just fine; indeed, he could do it all but blindfolded. The rewards of his and his wife's dual incomes were many. But finally he had to face up to the fact that he had no passion for his own daily grind.

Just as Jeff Gray felt about his consulting career, so Richard felt about his controller work: He was on a lifetime treadmill, a hamster in a business suit. And so, in trying to figure out how to escape this golden trap, he had a conversation with himself about what his goals should be, what "success" truly meant to him, and where he wanted his life's journey to lead.

Burkina Faso had been in turmoil when Richard was there, and it was still recovering from an uprising that had ended the nation's days as Upper Volta. Nonetheless, Richard had loved the Peace Corps and the challenges and the daily satisfaction of teaching people whose need was so obvious and close to the surface. What's more, he had been demonstrably good at the work and far more energized by it than by anything he had tried since. That's what he set out to recapture.

Returning to the Peace Corps as a field worker was unrealistic in personal and family terms. Richard was in his midforties by then, and his daughter was still in elementary school. Instead, he focused on the one career that he thought would best merge his obvious passions and strengths for this new phase of his life: teaching.

Over the course of three years, Richard segued from a full-time employee taking night courses in graduate education to a full-time student, and finally to his own classroom. Today, six years after slowly launching himself into the unknown, Richard is the history department chairman at DC's only honors high school—highly regarded, bringing hope to a desperately challenged public-school system, and more fulfilled than he has ever been in his life.

In the odd, circular path such stories often take, he was invited to Africa in the summer of 2007 to spend a month participating in a seminar—back to the place where he had the first hints of a calling that took him two decades to find.

Richard and Andy were both thoroughly ordinary working stiffs until they found the exact point at which their competencies aligned. Then, commitment flourished. The passion leveraged innate strengths, and the successful exercise of innate strengths fueled the passion. Andy cared deeply about music but wasn't utilizing his true talents. Richard was skilled at his career but lacked zeal. One found a solution waiting just around the bend. The other reshaped past experience to fit present realities and create a path to a fulfilling future. In each case, once passion and talent merged and began feeding off one another, their ultimate potential was unlocked.

Andy was already a solo act. He had to create a venue to let his competencies shine forth. Richard was in the wrong field, doing the wrong work. Like many of the others profiled in this book, he had to redefine not just his work life but his sense of calling. Neither Andy nor Richard found success and fulfillment by triumphing in some Darwinian up-or-out struggle. (And, in fact, as we'll see in future chapters, an up-or-out struggle isn't even Darwinism.) Rather, they found their success and fulfillment by maximizing what was already present and unique in each of them. And so can you.

The Primary Color Assessment

Through the process of finding your Primary Color, you come to understand the roots of your job performance and satisfaction, and can predict the level of your success and fulfillment if you follow your current path. But organizations also can gain incredibly valuable insights from a true understanding of the unique competencies of their workforce. Through an understanding of Primary Colors, companies can unlock the potential of their personnel, especially those whose job assignments fail to leverage their skills and passion. Repositioning employees and structuring career paths to take advantage of each individual's Primary Color can create real and tangible gains in productivity, performance, and morale.

Whether you are an employer or an employee, a boss or a cog, try asking yourself this simple set of questions: If tomorrow you woke up and had more positive energy and passion for your work and family, how significantly would that change your life for the better? As a leader, how valuable would it be to bring positive energy to the workforce? If those you lead could call on more positive energy, how would it impact their relationships with each other, and your entire organization?"

Those are the issues at play here. And that gets us to the test itself.

This is an Internet test. To access it, go to www.primary colorassessment.com. Log on to that site by providing a valid email address. There you will find an extensive explanation of the test and tool. I'll summarize it here for the curious . . . and wary.

Part 1 consists of three batteries of questions. For each set of questions, you will be asked to select "most like me," "least like me," or neither. The goal is for you to select among similar but subtly different statements. Doing so allows the Internet tool to understand your preferences, strengths, and priorities. From this, you will be given a Primary Color—one of dozens of different possibilities, for reasons that are explained online. You will also get an explanation about what your unique color means for you.

Part 2 of the test involves a shorter series of questions about your job. From this, you will be provided with a higher-level understanding of where your current work lies on the spectrum, pointing you to broader areas of the overall chart—what I call "color clusters". The distance between where you are (point A) and where your Primary Color lies (point B) implies the length of the journey ahead, but keep in mind that this is almost certainly a false measure. What matters isn't the distance between A and B; what counts is the direction in which your career is moving.

Once you complete the Primary Color Assessment, you will receive your Primary Color—your strongest point of preference, passion, and competency—as well as an online guide explaining how your color is likely to express itself in real-world situations. But don't stress out. This is one test that can never be passed or failed. No Primary Color is better than any other. Nor is there an ideal outcome except for the window you gain into your competencies and preferences that can positively change the way you look at the world forever!

But there's more to the leap than this. This is literally news you can use, but until you set it in motion, finding your Primary Color amounts to little more than wasted potential.

My Leap Journal—
What Is My Primary Color?

What did the online assessment tool tell me was my Primary Color? What parts of the description were clearly accurate? What surprised me?

Is my current job aligned with my Primary Color? If not, what simple things can I do now to better match my day-to-day activities with my strengths and passions?

Is my career steering me toward, around, or away from my Primary Color? Does my career trajectory seem correct, need slight course correction, or require a major overhaul?

Big, Selfless, and Simple: How Ideas Become Contagious

6

By the fall of 1984, the career of British punk rocker Bob Geldof was about as flatlined and rut-stuck as you can get in the rarified air of rock 'n' roll. While his band, the Boomtown Rats, had had some regional success in the United Kingdom, none of its songs had climbed higher than number 67 on the U.S. charts. Far too often, Geldof's music and the Rats' performances ended on a sour note.

One seemingly promising single, "I Don't Like Mondays," no sooner hit the airwaves than it was boycotted by the radio industry after word leaked out that Geldof had written the song about a woman shooting school children from her apartment window. Geldof's antics also had angered numerous local governments, many of whom now refused to issue permits to clubs if the Rats were planning to play there. And his record label informed him they had little interest in his band yet wouldn't release the Rats from their contract—a crippling situation referred to in the music industry as "shelving."

Geldof had once grandly declared that his goals in life were to "get rich, get famous, and get laid." Instead, he was broke, fast fading from public memory, and completely alone. Then one dreary London evening in mid-November 1984, as he sat slouched in front of his television, BBC aired a documentary about a hundred-year drought that was threatening millions of Ethiopians with starvation.

Geldof would later recall that he was transformed by the BBC program; his personal worries disappeared, replaced by an overwhelming need to do something. The next day Geldof began calling fellow musicians, suggesting a group single to benefit starvation victims. The task was an uphill one—he had strained relationships with just about everyone—but with the passion of the idea behind him, he was able to pull together the core of British rock royalty in only three weeks to record "Do They Know It's Christmas?" Quickly released, the record generated hundreds of thousands of dollars for famine relief.

But the momentum didn't stop there. Geldof's simple and oft-repeated plea that "everyone can do something" soon caught on with the British public and across Western Europe. Bakers began donating food. Schools held canned-goods drives. Children were knitting blankets. Almost like a spiraling contagion, people throughout the United Kingdom and Europe enlisted in the cause.

As the momentum began to spread to America, Geldof latched on to an even bigger idea. Why not host the largest concert in the history of the world in support of this cause? Conceived in January 1985, Live Aid was successfully birthed less than 7 months later, on July 13.

The fact is that absolutely nothing in the history of entertainment—not Woodstock or any other mass event—comes anywhere near matching Live Aid in scope, in numbers, in impact, or in the grandeur of its concept. Staged primarily at two locations—Wembley Stadium in London and Philadelphia's JFK Stadium—the concert was broadcast globally in real time in one of the largest TV satellite linkups ever. An estimated 1.5 billion viewers in 100 countries watched at least some part of the 16 hours' worth of performances.

Highlights included performances by Elvis Costello; U2; The Who; Elton John; Paul McCartney, singing an equipment-malfunction-plagued "Let It Be"; Crosby, Stills, and Nash; the Beach Boys; Santana; Tom Petty; Neil Young; Eric Clapton; Led Zeppelin; Duran Duran, in the last performance of the original band members; and Bob Dylan. At Wembley, Phil Collins soloed and joined Sting for a pair of duets before hopping on a Concorde, flying to Philadelphia, and performing again at JFK.

Contributions were solicited throughout the show. When the final tally was in, Live Aid had raised a little over $245 million from every corner of the world. Not one of the entertainers who helped raise the money was paid a dime for his or her time.

How did something so epic happen so quickly? How was Bob Geldof, stuck in the very trough of his life, able to bring together such a massive and diverse group—people of every ethnic, religious, and economic background, and citizens of more than 100 countries—unite them in common cause, and accomplish in such a brief time one of the greatest entertainment feats in the history of the planet?

To be sure, Live Aid would transform Geldof's career and life from ordinary to extraordinary, but it certainly wasn't the decidedly nonmagnetic force of his personality or his limited (and often strained) contacts or virtually nonexistent stature within the industry that launched the global cascade that became the unparalleled worldwide phenomenon of Live Aid.

Nor can the phenomenon be explained solely by the voluntary participation of so many of the rock world's most famous acts, or by the high drama of the cause, or even by Geldof's direct plea to help. All those elements helped raise the profile of the event. They gave it emotional content and drama. But celebrities volunteering their time for good causes is nothing new. They've been doing that since long before Jerry Lewis started his famous telethons.

Famine, alas, is nothing new either. Within the living memory of most of us, millions have died of starvation in Africa, and millions more are constantly threatened. CARE and other groups frequently call our attention to the desperate there, yet most of us manage to turn our attention away without contributing, without getting involved, without in many cases even giving the reality of mass starvation much of a second thought.

This time, though, the world didn't turn away. Why? What was it about Live Aid that so caught the world's attention that one-third of all the people alive on the planet would tune in to watch it and collectively donate just shy of a quarter billion dollars to the cause?

Why is it that some ideas take flight and spread like wildfire, while others, seemingly equally unique or worthy, fall mostly on deaf ears?

Big, Selfless, and Simple

It turns out that all ideas are not created equal. Just as some species share traits that make them more likely to spread through evolution—enjoyable orgasms is one, for obvious reasons—so some ideas have traits that put them at a distinct advantage to captivate and spread.

Big ideas get noticed; they break through the brain's natural barrier to noise and clutter and get us to pay attention. Selfless ones appeal to our very deeply seated sense of empathy and actually create a physiological urge to sign on. Simple ideas spread quickly because they are easy to grasp and easily translated into action by others.

In concert, big, selfless, and simple ideas attract, inspire, and involve others, and create a multiplier effect that can result in broad achievement beyond what any one person could hope to accomplish alone. Rather than depend on the precious few for validation, big, selfless, and simple ideas come with their own broadly based chorus of champions.

The Global Cascade

For at least two decades, accepted wisdom has held that trends are launched by a narrow band of highly informed and persuasive—influential—individuals to whom others look for guidance and direction. Often called "early adopters," or "connectors," these influentials are supposed to act essentially like disease vectors, infecting those around them with new ideas or a thirst for new products that then spreads epidemic-like through all of society.

Marketers naturally have courted influentials, even coddled them. In their 1997 book *The 500-Year Delta*, marketing gurus Jim Taylor and Watts Wacker recount the story of a major clothing line that was suffering heavy losses from shoplifting at its brand-name urban stores. No sooner would a new line of jeans hit the shelves than inner-city male teens would begin carrying them out of the store without paying. What to do?

Taylor and Wacker note approvingly that the company, in fact, did nothing at all. These teens were the early adopters. What they wore ended up in MTV videos. What appeared in MTV videos created a market demand that would spread to suburban malls and soon sweep the nation. Far from being a problem, these nimble-fingered urban youth appeared to be a marketer's dream: self-identifying influentials who walked into the store and helped themselves.

Maybe, but new research suggests that what the company was doing was encouraging shoplifting. Columbia University sociologists Duncan Watts and Peter Dodds have called into serious question both the power of influentials and the entire marketing approach built around them. Watts and Dodds don't discount the power of outsized personalities to launch products—Oprah Winfrey's book club, for example—but such instances, they argue, are relatively few and far between.

For early adopters, launching social epidemics depends upon the same dynamic as chain letters, or a Ponzi scheme: Person A sends the letter to ten people. Each of those ten people sends it to ten more each, and so on. That works fine so long as everyone cooperates, but all it takes to disrupt the cascade effect is a relatively low percentage of people at each step along the way who simply won't take part. In this way, the chain is broken, or in Ponzi terms, the last sucker is never found.

Using thousands of computer simulations, Watts and Dodds found that the prime requirement for what they call "global cascades" is not a few influentials but their polar opposite: a "critical mass of influenced people, each of whom adopts, say, a look or a brand after being exposed to a single adopting neighbor."

As Watts and Dobbs write, it's not who lights the initial spark that determines how wide a forest fire will spread, but the state of the forest itself—dry or wet, underbrush or no underbrush, and so on. In other words, it is not necessarily the source of the idea, but people's degree of receptivity to it that matters most. "If the network permits global cascades because it has the right concentration and configuration of adopters, virtually anyone can start one. If it doesn't permit cascades, nobody can."

Ideas that are contagious take advantage of this basic principle—they share common characteristics that make them much more likely to be received, acted upon, and spread. Even in the roar of the crowd, they are easily heard. They invoke proactive empathy because their selflessness draws people out of their own concerns and melts away indifference across broad swaths of society. In a world of ever-increasing complexity, big, selfless, and simple ideas are the one true, clear, and readily actionable thing we all long for.

Instead of disease vectors, ideas that catch hold and spread quickly should be thought of as viruses: big enough to overcome the amazingly complex defenses our bodies throw at them, so selfless that they can spread quickly to others, and simple enough to mutate with ease and catch hold even in hostile environments. The bottom line is this: get the idea right, and a global cascade will build all on its own.

For evidence, let's look more closely at Bob Geldof and Live Aid.

- Live Aid was *big*. Geldof referred to it as a "global jukebox." Whatever you call it, this was the single most participative event in the history of humankind, and it was staged to confront what would have been one of the largest mass starvations in modern times. Both qualities made it impossible to ignore.

- Live Aid was *selfless*. Part of that was because of the performers. Some of the most recognizable people in the world came together, without reward, to benefit some of the world's poorest people, and the world responded in kind. But the larger part by far was the cause itself. Having gained the world's attention through the sheer audacity of its size and ambition, Live Aid focused it on the plight of fellow human beings almost certain to die if no help was forthcoming. Inevitably, that invoked empathy at the individual and global levels, and empathy compelled people to watch and, in many cases, act.

- Live Aid was also surprisingly *simple*. Having captured the world's attention and focused it on desperate people in specific need, Geldof offered an easy way to participate in the solution: "Everyone can do something, no matter how big or small. Just do something." To the royal family of Dubai, that meant contributing £1 million to the cause. Others gave $5 or $10 or even less. Still others, rich and poor, young and old, contributed in-kind goods and services. Whatever the amount or its form, the participation was an easily accomplished response to what is in reality a painfully intractable set of problems.

Three words—Big. Selfless. Simple—hold the key to the leap, to translating the energy that comes with finding your Primary Color into an actionable plan.

That's how you get heard when everyone around you is shouting. That's how you make common cause with the angels and align your Primary Color with something worthy of the discovery. And that, finally, is how you corral your own chorus of champions and launch a global cascade. These aren't simply ideas—ideas are a dime a dozen. These are infectious ideas that the world feels compelled to adopt and act on.

Big Ideas

As we've just seen, the order is important. Big comes first.

Big ideas break through our very powerful attention barrier and create the opportunity for consideration.

A confession: once World50 was up and running, I spent the first year unwaveringly certain that it was going to work and every year since wondering how it ever did. Early on, I confided to one of our founding members that I couldn't fully explain how or why I had been successful.

"I'll tell you why," he said. "The reason this worked is that along with the invitation, you sent me a [bleeping] $50,000 invoice! That was more than twice what anything similar cost. My assistant always throws these invitations away, but this time she literally stormed into my office and said, *'Now, you've got to take a look at this!'* "

So, I'm extra-smart to have thought of that, right? No, not at all. I just stumbled by chance on to a passageway into our hard-to-reach brains.

The fact is, we don't succeed by paying attention to everything. We succeed for the most part by doing precisely the opposite—by letting go; by *not* paying conscious attention to the vast bulk of the data, sensations, and other impressions that come our way. The names of all the parts and functions of the brain that create and maintain barriers to our attention can be daunting: adaptive unconscious, ventromedial prefrontal cortex, amygdala, etc. The practical effect, though, is fairly straightforward: though we are flooded with data almost constantly, our brains generally focus on only about five pieces of information at a time.

The rest isn't necessarily lost—odd things come flying back at us from the memory bank, things we never knew had found a way in there—but if the information the brain is presented with has no immediacy or any other quality that makes it stand out from the crowd, chances are low that it will be moved to the relevant pile. And if it doesn't make that pile, chances of full engagement are almost zero.

With attention, it's quality, not quantity, that counts; it's what we notice, not how much we notice. That's what the $50,000 "invoice" I included with each World50 invitation assured: that my invitation would break out of the crowd, that attention would be paid. To be sure, the comparatively high fee was nothing more than brand positioning, but it aligned my pitch with the ancient architecture of the brain.

Eons of evolution have served to structure our brains to be

our own exquisite spam filter, filing cabinet, and dead-letter office. That's the keep-out function, the part of our brain that separates the little bit of relevant from the great mass of irrelevant. Without that filter, we would be swamped.

Even more important is the nonfilter function of our brain, the part that lets in the things we ultimately end up paying attention to. Here, priority ranking, speed of recognition, and speed of execution are everything.

Our ancestors 10,000 years ago didn't think, *Spotted hide, exceedingly long incisors, saber-toothed tiger, run!* They ran first, *then* realized what they were running from, and then finally, in their own primitive way, tried to draw a lesson from the experience. (*Tiger. Tar pit. Sundown. Bad!*) That's how they survived and ultimately prospered, by listening to the oldest part of the brain first—the fight-or-flee limbic system—then proceeding up the reasoning chain.

Very few of us in this day and age face a continuous string of daily life-and-death decisions, but whether it's commuting on the freeway, trading on the floor of the commodity or stock exchange, shopping, or just going about the daily business of life, we still retain the capacity *and* the inclination to make highly accurate and binding decisions in what amounts to a blink of the eye. (And indeed it was that capacity for virtually instantaneous and surprisingly accurate decision making that gave Malcolm Gladwell the title for his best-selling book— *Blink*.)

The main reason the tabloid and magazine covers in the racks by the supermarket checkout line are so lurid and bright and show so much flesh is a simple matter of the time-brain interface. Studies show that consumers make newsstand buy–no buy decisions in two seconds or less. Tick-tock, and the sell opportunity is gone. This is what keeps the editors of newsstand-dependent publications awake late into the night.

Teachers might sleep less well, too, if they were more widely aware of a study by Nalini Ambady and Robert Rosenthal that gauged how long students needed to measure classroom effectiveness. One group of students saw fairly lengthy video segments of teachers performing in front of full classrooms. The other group saw only two seconds of the same videos—the same span as the buy–no buy decision mentioned earlier. The rest they had to extrapolate from their experience over the years with their own teachers. When the two groups were asked to rank and evaluate the teachers they had just seen, they arrived at remarkably similar results.

In part, then, big ideas have an advantage over smaller ones for a very obvious reason: in a world of snap judgments, big ideas are easier to notice, and their very bigness gives them an immediacy that smaller ideas lack. The immediacy, in turn, pushes other, competing considerations to the background. Just as the body in extreme stress begins to shunt blood toward the vital organs, so the brain under stress concentrates its attention on what it perceives to be the task most at hand.

That was Live Aid's initial advantage. Even in a world in which attention windows are shrunk to two seconds, Geldof's audacious plan to stage the grandest event the world had ever known and relieve famine in Ethiopia was so impossible to ignore that it crowded out other ideas competing for a hearing on the global stage.

Sara Blakely accomplished the same thing by insisting, first to herself and later to store buyers and customers, that she was creating not just a new product but an entirely new category—women's clothing that was different in kind and origin, not just in degree. Like new ideas, new products are everywhere. The stores are packed with them. But new *categories* come along only once in a blue moon. Their rarity makes them the big idea that crowds out all the little ones clamoring for a hearing.

Breaking the attention barrier, though, only gets an idea to the starting line.

Selfless Ideas

Selfless ideas evoke empathy. By stirring us to action and increasing our willingness to engage, they create a contagion that causes them to spread.

In 2002, Silvia Lagnado was faced with one of the largest challenges of her emerging career at Unilever. Soft-spoken and far more likely to tout others' accomplishments than her own, Silvia comes across as exactly the opposite of the Type A personalities who tend to dominate corporate wars. Now, she found herself right in the middle of one.

A year earlier, Unilever had embraced the idea of global brand teams and named Silvia to lead the six-person group in charge of one of the company's most important brands: Dove. On paper, that gave Silvia serious clout. The reality, though, was far different.

Launched in 1872 in the Netherlands, Unilever grew up on a culture of independence and decentralization and still held fiercely to both. Thus, although Silvia was managing the Dove brand on a global basis, she had, in effect, almost no resources globally or locally on her side. Nor was there conspicuous enthusiasm for the branding concept that Silvia's team began cautiously floating around the company—that Dove should be celebrating "real beauty."

Silvia, though, became convinced that the entire campaign should be built around everyday women of all shapes and sizes celebrating their own beauty and not being ashamed by it. To her, the idea was absolutely compelling, the internal battle worth it, and the need manifest.

The statistics on women, beauty, and self-perception are well-known and globally alarming. Only 13 percent of women around the world say they are very satisfied with their weight and shape. Just 2 percent of women globally consider themselves beautiful, and more than half say their bodies disgust them. As many as 10 percent of all U.S, college females suffer from at least borderline eating disorders, and half of those have clinical bulimia nervosa. In the United Kingdom, about 5 percent of secondary-school girls suffer from anorexia.

The root causes of this pandemic of dieting and body self-loathing are about as well-known as the manifestations: a fashion industry that worships at the altar of unattainable beauty; runway models with sunken eyes and a wraithlike thinness that for the vast majority of women can be achieved only through starvation dieting, forced vomiting, chain-smoking, or worse; and advertising meant to make women aspire to a look that virtually no healthy woman can achieve. (This is the industry, remember, that invented Kate Moss and "heroin chic.")

All this drove Silvia and her team on; they had motivation to burn. But motivation alone wasn't going to carry the day against a deeply entrenched corporate culture and mind-set—indeed, a mind-set that had helped create the very conditions she was reacting against.

"We made the claim to management that 'we are going to transform the brand' and that we would do this using real women—of every shape and size—in our ads," she says. "But for the first six months, we were not able to generate any significant momentum internally."

To get the upper hand against such long odds, Silvia and her team did what undermanned armies often resort to. They initiated what proved to be a magnificent piece of guerrilla warfare.

"We didn't have any advertising, and we needed to get some senior people involved to push this forward, so in each country we secretly filmed the young daughters of C-level executives. We asked them what they didn't like about their bodies. We told them they could name one thing only. I don't like my freckles, my hair, my butt. I'm too heavy, I'm too short."

I'm ugly.

"Then we added music and played it back to the people whose daughters we had filmed. Here were grown men sitting in a wood-paneled executive conference room, watching their own preteen daughters, cute young girls, saying that they didn't feel pretty—slender ten-year-olds saying that they were fat. It was as emotional and powerful as you could get. There consistently was stony silence that would fill the room, most often followed by tears. It was uncomfortable, but they got it."

And with the inevitability of a rising tide, the ad concept gelled. In an industry famous for aspirational ads, these were inspirational in the extreme, simple visuals that managed to summon a range of emotions that would have done a two-hour feature film proud. The campaign didn't have to look for empathy. Empathy came running to the concept, first and foremost from inside the company.

"We could tell whenever we got people in a room and talked about this that we had a big idea here. We initially had nothing really but an idea, but the amount of enthusiasm was amazing."

Most important, the ads just plain worked, ultimately launching what amounted to a global Dove Campaign for Real Beauty lovefest. Most marketing ideas are push, push, push. But once this campaign hit critical mass, the compasses all aligned, and it was pull, pull, pull all the way.

Because the ads tapped so deeply into the hearts and minds and personal histories of so many girls and women, they had to be shown a relatively few times to create a social contagion. And because the follow-up has been so thorough and in many ways so ingenious, the contagion has continued to spread three years after the first ad was shown.

One of the most remarkable by-products of this campaign has been a short video titled "Evolution" that shows, at breakneck speed, an attractive but unglamorous young girl being made up and retouched in photographs (freckles erased, eyes widened, neck stretched) until she appears totally glamorous on a billboard at the end. The caption is at once instructive, uplifting, and fundamentally simple—"No wonder our perception of beauty is distorted"—but what has been truly amazing is the video's shelf life. First posted on YouTube in October 2006, "Evolution" was seen by 6 million online viewers in its first 16 months, an average of 13,000 YouTube viewers a day, for which Dove has had to pay the same thing Bob Geldof had to pay his Live Aid performers: not a single thin dime.

Unilever is not a charity. It's a global enterprise operating in 150 countries around the world. The goal of Silvia Lagnado and her Dove brand team was never *not* to move product. Unilever is, like other companies, focused on sales and shareholders.

But by looking at the challenge through a selfless as well as a market lens, Silvia and her team broadened the base of support for Dove beyond anything that could have been accomplished through market transactions alone. They weren't just selling soaps or creams or lotions; at heart, they were selling a feeling about "real beauty" that any woman—and any Dove or Unilever employee, for that matter—could fashion his or her own value proposition around. And by doing that—by building the Campaign for Real Beauty around an idea that was truly selfless—Silvia and her team did more than move product; they moved an industry.

Today, Unilever has a corporate-wide strategy launched directly from the office of the CEO encouraging all its employees to look at decisions not just in economic terms, but also in terms of the social and environmental impact that a brand can have.

Today, too, Silvia Lagnado, who launched the Campaign for Real Beauty from a very ordinary rear seat far back in the peanut gallery of the Unilever hierarchy, is on an extraordinary career arc at the company. Six years after using her very tenuous middle manager's position to subvert and ultimately overthrow key elements of an engrained corporate culture, Silvia is a senior vice president in charge of the company's leading brands.

This is the transformative effect of a selfless idea—on careers, on callings, even on entrenched organizations. And it happens time and again.

Live Aid broke the attention barrier by being loud—think amps the size of small office towers—and by boldly tackling a giant problem. But Live Aid engaged and created contagion by being selfless. The event featured some of the most raging egos in the entertainment world, but it was never about them. Instead, it was about simply doing the right thing for people who needed the right thing so badly. Just as Dove's Real Beauty campaign was pointed outward toward women who had suffered for untold decades from the advertising of the beauty industry, so Live Aid was directed outward toward the famine victims, not pointed inward toward its famous and not-so-famous principals. And that's what made the difference ultimately: its selflessness transformed Live Aid from a global concert to a global cascade.

Sara Blakely's SPANX or Jeff Gray's 180-Degree Kitchen or Brad Margus's Perlegen Sciences or even my w50 don't swim in the same river as Live Aid or Real Beauty. Geldof and Silvia Lagnado took on the planet. We just took on corners of it. Some of our ideas were for profit; others were not. Some of us drove our goals forward by the force of our personalities—Sara Blakely most notably. Others tried to disappear into the idea itself. I intentionally branded everything related to World50 white. Even the text was white on white—so white, in fact, that my dad complains he can hardly see it. But I wanted the message to quietly scream, "It's not about me; it's about our customers!"

In every case, whether we were in it for profit or not, we set out to meet a need that wasn't being served. Our efforts were directed singularly at the cause, while our own hopes took a backseat. I started a business for a group that had no existing mechanism to come together to share common experiences. Sara created a fashion category built specifically around the needs of women, far from typical in a male-dominated industry. That was our "selflessness," and that's why people responded as they did.

Think of Steve Jobs. He has made literally billions of dollars simply by building products that he felt should exist. Customers and even employees are deeply devoted to Apple because they perceive it as being about the cause—about taking on self-serving corporations that force their products on us and instead delivering what customers really want. That, too, is selflessness, and selflessness is what gives big ideas the legs to run with.

Selfless ideas literally draw us out of our own concerns, and out of the self-absorption that is the single biggest impediment to shared action. When we focus on ourselves, our world narrows, and problems and preoccupations loom large. When we focus on others, our own problems drift to the periphery, and we increase our capacity for connection and compassionate action.

This is not a new observation. The Bible, Shakespeare, the great works of other cultures are replete with examples of the stirring power of selflessness. In *The Happiness Hypothesis*, Jonathan Haidt cites Thomas Jefferson on the subject: "When any . . . act of charity or of gratitude, for instance, is presented either to our sight or imagination, we are deeply impressed with its beauty and feel a strong desire in ourselves of doing charitable and grateful acts also."

Jefferson went on to record with considerable accuracy the physical effect that comes from encountering acts of generosity even at second hand: "The reader's breast dilates. His sentiments are elevated as much as any similar event in the real world can elevate them. We feel like a better person when we hear of such incidents, and we are inclined to act like one as well."

Psychologists today can point to endless studies on selflessness, empathy, and their effects, but almost inevitably contemporary professionals in the field end up using the same basic language set as Jefferson when they talk about "elevation" and its contagious effect on those who witness brave or kind or stirring deeds. To see someone dash into a building on the edge of collapse increases our own propensity to do the same—9/11 was full of such examples. Similarly, to see or hear people give money encourages us to pull out our own checkbooks—that's the psychology behind the fund-raising weeks on public radio and TV.

Empathy isn't just in our head. It spreads through our whole body. Jonathan Haidt writes about one of his undergraduate honors students who, for her thesis, brought 45 lactating women with babies into the lab, one at time. All the women were asked to put nursing pads into their bras. Half the mothers were shown a film clip from an *Oprah* show in which a musician first expressed gratitude to his own music teacher for rescuing him from a life of gang crime, then was presented with a sampling of his own students expressing gratitude to him. The other half watched a clip featuring a number of comedians. Afterward, both sets of mothers and their babies were left alone in a viewing room for five minutes.

To no one's surprise, the mothers who had seen the stirring clip about the musician fed their babies or simply leaked milk far more freely than those who had merely been entertained by the comedy sampling. They also cuddled or otherwise touched their babies far more often, in warmer ways. This is what empathy does: it triggers compassion. It compels us to give back—in a nursing mother's case, literally in the form of lactation.

And notice that these mothers were not watching Geldof try to save the world; they were simply observing a group showing gratitude. It turns out that even these minor acts of selflessness, whether showing gratitude or even authentically meeting a customer need, trigger the same physiological reactions and at the same levels as observing someone trying to save the world.

Darwin, too, addressed the subject when he speculated that every emotion predisposes us to act in a unique way. When we encounter anger, we are inclined to react with anger. When we hear a scream of anguish or perceive someone is trying to help us or others, empathy is invoked within us. To see or hear, Darwin thought, readies us to do in like fashion.

As so often happens with Darwin's theories, what he guessed at has since been largely confirmed. Brain imaging shows that the neural networks for perception and action share a common code in the language of the brain. To feel any emotion does, in fact, stir the related urge to act. We see Geldof helping, and we instinctively pitch in. We perceive that Steve Jobs made the iPod specifically for "me," and we want to tell everyone else about it.

Panty hose that make you look better, a leg up for the homeless, a glimmer of hope for genetic diseases, peer-to-peer support, Live Aid, the Campaign for Real Beauty—they were all outward-directed big ideas that broke the attention barrier and then effortlessly drew others into the campaign. People noticed us; they lived inside the problems that our ideas were helping them solve; and the ideas spread and morphed into a movement. That got us to Stage 2, but there was still one more hurdle for our ideas to clear.

Simple Ideas

Simple ideas are easy to grasp and translate into action, increasing the odds that people actually will respond.

A literary-agent friend likes to talk about what he calls the "elevator speech" test. Assume for a moment that you are in midtown Manhattan about to pitch a book. Further assume that by sheer chance, you arrive at your destination, step into the elevator, and find yourself all alone with the editor in chief of whatever publishing house you have come to see. You now have 60 floors to sell the book. Can you do it?

"If the title isn't immediately clear by the fifteenth floor, the book is toast," my friend says. "It doesn't have to be the final title, it just has to be easy to grasp. After that, you've got 30 floors to sell the premise, and this is an express elevator. No one else is getting in or out. That leaves you another 15 floors to sell the author's credentials and make this editor in chief want to see his logo on the book spine.

"If you can do all that, the book will be lodged in her brain, and you can follow up in a few days and she'll still know what you're talking about. If you haven't made the elevator sale, she'll forget about your book while she's walking down the hall to her office."

We can quibble over the floor count allocation and the total time it takes an elevator to climb 60 floors, but the basic premise holds. Complex ideas, whether theories or propositions, engage the intellect and rouse contemplation, but they are rarely goads to immediate action. Simple ideas, by contrast, anchor themselves in our consciousness and memory.

Consider, for example, what neuroscientists refer to as

"earworms"—those snatches of song that get stuck in your memory bank and play over and over again, sometimes annoyingly so. Unless you're a professional musician, these earworms are rarely long and almost never comprised of anything more than a simple melody. Research shows that the average auditory memory capacity maxes out at about 30 seconds; thus, by their very simplicity and ease of memorization, earworms become embedded, making them more likely to catch on and almost impossible to shake out.

In a similar vein, lists of simple words are also easier to remember than lists of longer ones. In fact, the breakeven point is about the same two seconds that we need to make buy–no buy, good–no good decisions. If a word takes longer to articulate than that, the memory bank tends to spit it out. With the brain, two seconds seems to be a magic number.

A closely related advantage of simplicity is that it allows action to be very easily and personally translated, which almost exponentially increases the chances of participation. Why? Because you're not asking people to fill a particular niche in a complicated response strategy. You are asking only that they take part. The absence of specific direction allows them to shape their response in accord with their own means, talents, and interests. In effect, participants can take possession of their own contribution to the cause.

I'm reminded of the time President John F. Kennedy visited what was then called Cape Canaveral, in Florida. Kennedy, you may recall, had promised during the 1960 presidential campaign to place a man on the moon before the end of the decade. Now, on a trip to the NASA launch site to check on the space agency's progress, he engaged a janitor in conversation.

"What are you up to?" the president inquired.

"I'm taking us to the moon," the janitor replied proudly, and in his own mind—because the mandate had been so simple and broadly writ—that's exactly what he was doing.

Bob Geldof's broad appeal to "do something. . . . Just do something" shares the same genius. It gave people license to do almost anything. Yes, most gave money, but seamstresses hemmed, bread makers baked, lighting technicians wired the performance venues in London and Philadelphia, sound technicians looked after the amps and the live feed, and on and on. Geldof's message was simple: people are starving right now. And the translation was both equally simple and immensely inviting: do (literally) whatever you can do.

Without realizing it, I basically did the same thing with w50. My idea, and indeed the entire original proposition, was merely that the top 50 chief marketing officers would get together twice a year, with everyone kicking in $50,000 to the pot to make this happen, *and boy, won't it be cool!* That was it—nothing else—because, in truth, I hadn't yet fully fleshed out the idea beyond that point. But the unintended consequence of my vagaries was that, without specific direction on my end, the members each conjured up in their minds what they thought this would and should be. *Cool* is a broadly translated term.

We were all pulling in the same direction: improving peer-to-peer connection. Everyone wanted to expand the gene pool of ideas they could take back to their own companies. But the 50 members were encouraged to sign on because they would bring 50 different and highly individual value propositions to the table. That never would have happened if I had shipped each of them in advance a business plan that laid out chapter and verse of organizational activities. Besides, as the old military maxim holds, no plan survives first contact in any event.

In Influence: *The Psychology of Persuasion*, Robert Cialdini cites a study in which a group of randomly chosen people were shown two print ads for the same product. One ad scrimped on positive details about the product; the other was brimming with them. Amazingly (but really not so), the bare-bones ad was judged by the ad hoc panel to be far more persuasive than the one with a longer list of compelling attributes. Why? Because the less you tell people, the more they can write themselves into the story.

As I write this, Apple is doing the same thing with its TV ad campaign for iPod. The music is neat. The dancing people are clearly happy. And all the viewer sees or hears or knows about the product is the logo that flashes briefly on the screen at the end. The ad is nothing more than an invitation to the join the iPod party. What you bring, what you wear, what you play—it's all up to you.

Sara Blakely told me not long ago that when she first starting selling fax machines and knew almost nothing about the product, her sales had been off the charts. Then, as she learned more about the machines she was selling and her sales pitch became more nuanced and detailed, her sales began to tail off. So she dumbed her pitch back down, and—voilà!—sales began to climb again. By resimplifying her approach, Sara was once again allowing her customers to envision the role of this fax machine in their lives rather than telling them what that match would be.

With ideas, less really is more. It's what *isn't* there that encourages participation and launches crusades.

Truth at 2,000 Times a Second

As A.K. Pradeep tells the story, his moment of great revelation into the deep workings of the brain came on a flight from Chicago to San Francisco in the summer of 2002. A long-time marketing consultant, Pradeep had spent the entire day with one of his most valued clients, the chief marketing officer of a global Fortune 500 company. As were almost all his clients, this one was frustrated by the inability to predict which messages will grab consumers' attention and stick, and which will fly right by them.

"What's wrong with them [consumers]?" his client moaned as Pradeep was leaving.

That lament was still ringing in Pradeep's ears as he boarded the plane and fell into small talk with his seatmate, a slightly disheveled, scholarly looking man in his early sixties who turned out to be a neuroscientist.

"I plug people in and study the workings of their brains," he explained to Pradeep. "Specifically, my team and I are conducting groundbreaking research in two areas. First, we're looking at children with ADD and ADHD, examining why some things can grab and hold their attention, while most things won't. We're also studying Alzheimer's patients, seeking to understand why certain things are held comfortably in their memory, while other thoughts and images quickly vanish. We are using the results to identify drug sets that will work most effectively."

In that moment, Pradeep says, he suddenly had the answer to his client's question. What's wrong with consumers is that they have, in effect, both attention deficit disorder (*Why do they pay attention to some information but not to others?*) and a commercial form of Alzheimer's (*Why do some things stick and others fade from memory?*)

And thus was born NeuroFocus, the company Pradeep founded to apply the emerging technologies of cognitive neuroscience to marketing applications. Today, a little more than half a decade later, Pradeep and his company are pioneers in the brand new field of neuroeconomics.

To discover more about what Pradeep has been learning, I visited his offices in Berkeley, California, on a beautiful spring morning in 2008. The building sits inconspicuously among numerous warehouses and light-industrial buildings, but almost nothing is normal inside. I was greeted by two women in their late twenties—both stunningly attractive, seemingly straight out of the Robert Palmer video "Addicted to Love." They led me upstairs to Pradeep's own offices, a jumble of tables stacked with scientific books and journals, and what appeared to be complex and expensive technical equipment lined against almost every wall.

I had just started taking it all in when Pradeep came bursting around the corner. Middle-aged, of modest stature and Indian descent, he was strikingly dressed in solid purple pants and a screaming purple paisley jacket covered in sequins that looked for all the world as if he had bought it straight off the set of Prince's 1980s movie *Purple Rain*. A human force field, Pradeep launched right into telling me about his business.

"Traditional research on advertising effectiveness has for decades suffered from a fundamental flaw," he said. "It relies on consumers themselves to articulate their feelings and emotions. Humans are very, very bad at articulating feelings and emotions."

Pradeep and his assistants took me to one of the testing rooms—a cubicle about six feet square with curtains draped on the walls and, at the center, a plush leather chair that I was told to sit in. A few feet in front of me was a television. A camera with two lenses sat just below the television. Another camera was mounted on a stand to the left of the TV, and cameras hung in each of the top corners of the room. All of them were pointed directly at me.

With what seemed like military precision, one of Pradeep's assistants covered my hair with a kind of light blue rubber swim cap perforated with colorful holes, then squirted something cold and oozy through the holes, and snapped in dozens of sensors. She then taped a few more sensors to my forehead. This wasn't the full load—sometimes, test subjects get up to 128 sensors, measuring 16 discrete processing sections of the brain at one time, but it was enough to make me feel strangely vulnerable and exposed.

"Now you are, as we say, capped," Pradeep told me. "With this, we can measure nearly everything. The brain sensors take a snapshot of brain activity 2,000 times every second. The forward camera directly in front of you measures not only eye movement but pupil dilation as well. The sensors on the forehead measure subtle messages from the skin, which typically occur four seconds after a stimulus. And with the camera in the corner and those near the ceiling, we are actually experimenting with the computer to identify and monitor specific facial expression sets."

Pradeep's team refers to this as "truth at 2,000 times a second." And as I sat and watched a 30-second TV spot, I found myself wondering what 60,000 truths were being revealed about me. The ad was an iPod commercial that showed the torso of an attractive woman lifting her shirt up and over her head to reveal a handsome man, who then lifted his shirt up and over his head to reveal another beautiful woman.

I never did find out what I had revealed to my testers (although something I did triggered a burst of laughter from the team in the next room!), but if this had been an actual diagnostic and not a demonstration, my reactions would have been used along with many others to rate the ad on a numeric scale and then to break the ad down into its component parts and the brain's discrete reaction to each, in a practically millisecond by millisecond analysis. Not only can NeuroFocus made recommendations based on that, but the company also has developed an algorithm that can automatically shorten a 30-second ad to the most effective 15 seconds, based solely on the feedback from the brains that have reacted to it.

I'm frankly a sucker for cutting-edge research like this, and Pradeep was glad to accommodate me. But he is also an intensely curious man, so back in his office, he asked me to expand on why I had flown across the continent for a few hours of his time. That's when I told him basically everything that this chapter has been about.

"Over the last several years," I said, "I've identified and deeply studied dozens and dozens of cases of people leading seemingly ordinary lives who all of a sudden made a leap to accomplish great and extraordinary things. I have looked closely at numerous aspects, characteristics, and factors related to these transitions. One result of this research is that, while the leaps that each individual made are as unique as the persons themselves, the ideas driving them to extraordinary achievement have all shared the same fundamental characteristics."

"And what were these characteristics?" he asked, leaning back in his Aeron chair with a look of almost amused anticipation on this face.

"Each of these ideas was big, meaning it was starkly ambitious," I replied. "Each was selfless, meaning the ambition was about the idea, not the individual. And each was simple, with a compact message and few supporting details. Big, selfless, and simple."

With that, Pradeep slowly leaned back and stretched his arms above him, eventually resting them behind his head.

"Big, selfless, and simple," he finally said. "Why, of course they were!"

And that is when things *really* got interesting.

From Information to Advocacy and Community

Pradeep told me that his team has identified six distinct sequential stages that occur when an individual engages an idea. In the first stage, the brain gathers information. The second stage is about evaluation. The third is the transaction: do I act or not? Stage four is support. The fifth is advocacy, and the sixth is community—the idea becomes part of me and others.

Big, ambitious ideas, Pradeep explained, go well beyond simply providing information. They actually work to compress the amount of time the brain requires to get through all of these stages. They take you from information to advocacy and community much more quickly, and as such, they dramatically increase the odds that you will get there.

Meanwhile, selfless ideas engage one of the emotions our

brains most crave—self-worth. Getting there doesn't require quitting your job and joining a group intent on saving the planet. Even minor acts will create the same result, and indeed our brains search all day long for whatever tiny contributions it can find to create a sense of self-worth. The self-worth, in turn, anchors the ideas into the final, powerful stages of advocacy and community.

Simple ideas are important for a different set of reasons. The brain absolutely loves puzzles. It takes great joy in identifying and solving them—and the solving part is important. If a crossword puzzle, say, is too difficult, we don't enjoy it, nor do we take any pleasure in a puzzle with the answers already written in. The joy is in the solving itself. Simple ideas act as small puzzles, especially when some part of the idea has been left intentionally blank so we get to fill it from our own needs and experience. This is the lure of the iPod ads with no product information whatsoever, of songs with melodies but vague and ambiguous lyrics, or for that matter of the completely sketchy value proposition I created with World50. Additional information would have made the offer more complete, but it also would have removed the puzzle and thus ultimately made the proposition less alluring.

What's more, simple ideas, Pradeep explained, are actually processed in a different area of the brain than their more complex counterparts, a section that has an inherent bias to say *yes*. By way of example, he cited a common dilemma that has long puzzled marketers.

In a well-known test performed numerous times, people are asked if they would prefer $99 today or $100 tomorrow. A separate group is asked if it would rather receive $99 in 364 days, or $100 in 365 days. In the first instance, nearly everyone chooses to take the $99 today. But in the second, nearly everyone opts to wait an extra day for the $100. Why is the value of a dollar worth a different amount today versus a year from now?

Until recently, scientists and marketers had no answer, but a neuroscientist from Princeton has recently shown that these two decisions are made in entirely different areas of the brain. Choosing $99 today versus $100 tomorrow is what is known as a short-term reward response—a powerful response zone that overpowers other areas of reasoning when it's called into action. Making the same decision requires much more reasoning when the time frame presented is a year, not a day, and thus that decision is made in the section of the brain reserved for more complex cognitive processing.

This, in fact, is the power of the famous Kmart blue light special. An item that's going to be selling at 20 percent off for the next two weeks gives you options. You can buy it today, but you can also put it off and consider whether you really need it. But when the item is going to be on sale in this store only, and only for the next 60 minutes, the choice immediately is farmed out to your short-term reward response, and the deal becomes incredibly difficult to pass up.

It's also what Sara Blakely did when she grabbed the Neiman Marcus buyer by the hand and all but dragged her to the ladies' room so she could demonstrate how well SPANX fit. In effect, Sara was creating an environment of urgency that closed off longer term cognitive processes of the brain and brought into play, instead, the short-term reward response, with its inherent *yes* bias. And, of course, *yes* is just what she got.

For that matter, Bob Geldof did the same thing, too. Had he told people that the famine in Ethiopia was a horrendous situation requiring multiple steps to create an internationally based organization plus further steps to raise the necessary money and even more steps to convert the money to food and distribute the food to those who are on the edge of starvation, everyone probably would have understood what he was proposing but teasing action out of that cognitive recognition would have been as big a challenge for Geldof as it is for CARE or any other relief agency.

Instead, Geldof said (a) people are dying right now, and (b) I am asking you to do something right now. Thus he evoked the short-term reward response and, *wham*, performed what seemed to be a virtual miracle but which really was no miracle at all—only the highly predictable firing of neurons. Life leads us down wonderful byways if only we choose to follow them.

Process, Not Outcome

Big, selfless, and simple ideas work. They work at the emotional level. They feed into the architecture of the brain and the evolutionary experience that designed the architecture. They find their echo in the brain's own molecular makeup.

Because they create global cascades, these are ideas that can literally change the world and alter self-perception across huge swaths of the populace. Think Live Aid and the Dove Campaign for Real Beauty. But "big" can be smaller than that. The "selfless" test doesn't require you to imitate Mother Teresa; it asks only that you serve someone else's need before your own. That's what Andy Levine did with his floating rock concerts.

"Simple" can be literally as simple as launching a small

mom-and-pop foundation to raise money for a heartfelt cause. Look where that led Brad Margus.

As I have stressed throughout this book, the process is what counts. Get that right and the outcome will take care of itself. Until you translate your idea into action, though, nothing will happen. And that brings us to chapter 7.

My Leap Journal—
Big, Selfless, and Simple

Think of an idea that you are currently working on at your job. Consider doing this exercise as a team.

How can I make this idea bigger, more ambitious, really stretch?

How can I make this idea more outward facing, a quest for a solution rather than for personal or team success? Are there any social and environmental goals that can be added to existing economic ones? How can I further simplify the idea to its core message?

Now, repeat these same questions, this time focusing on a goal or aspiration you have for your life.

The Spark Sequence: Stacking the Deck

7

Finding your Primary Color releases the energy that lies within. Tying that energy to an idea that is big, selfless, and simple gives the energy form and direction and enlists others in your cause. The Spark Sequence—a series of low-danger, exploratory events—builds exposure to what might lie ahead and confidence in the skills to get there while simultaneously mitigating risk.

Mitigating risk? I confess when that possibility first occurred to me, I wondered if I hadn't gone round the bend. Isn't embracing risk what capitalism is all about? And aren't those who take on the greatest risks the ones with career trajectories that look like missile launches? In the *Let's Make a Deal* show of life, they're the ones who rush pell-mell through Door No. 3 while the rest of us cower at our microphones, torn between one chance at a new car and the two cracks at our very own goat.

Just look at Bill Gates. Or better yet, listen to the opening of the commencement address Gates delivered at Harvard University back in June 2007 when he was awarded an honorary law degree: "President Bok, members of the Harvard Corporation and the Board of Overseers, members of the faculty, parents, and especially, the graduates: I've been waiting more than 30 years to say this: 'Dad, I always told you I'd come back and get my degree!'"

Buried in those few modest words is an entire epic narrative of how the world's most famous college dropout became the world's richest man. You've undoubtedly heard it: Geeky kid comes from obscurity and gets accepted to Harvard. Then, throwing all caution to the wind, he gives up this once-in-a-lifetime shot to earn higher education's most coveted degree and instead drops out on a whim to start a company in an industry that doesn't even exist yet. Originally called Micro-Soft, the company struggles for several years but eventually grows into the world's largest corporation as measured by market capitalization, and Gates becomes not only the world's No. 1 rich guy but also one of global philanthropy's most generous patrons.

That's not risk mitigation. That's risk *aggravation*, and the underlying message is pretty clear: if you don't have the guts to play, get the heck out of the way. Certainly, that's the lesson I took away from it.

Putting All the Chips on the Table?

Growing up as I did, with an early interest in business, it was almost impossible not to envy people like Gates, and even measure myself against them. Gates had placed all his chips on the table at one time and walked away richer than Croesus. And me? Well, I'd never even sat down at the table. The way I saw it, I couldn't.

I graduated from a state university with a stack of loans to repay. No sooner had I begun to dig my way out of personal debt than I met my wife (who failed to bring her own shovel). I remember her father joking with me soon after we got engaged. "Son," he said, "I want to let you know about Lori's dowry—you get her student loans and her bad teeth!" He laughed from deep in his chest. I moaned from the same spot. Add to that three children born within five years, and I felt like I was slogging through quicksand.

If only I was in a different position, I used to think. If only I had the courage to take on more risk, like Gates, like lots of others I used to list to myself. And then finally, years later, I realized that that's not how it happened at all.

William Henry Gates III was born October 28, 1955, in Seattle, Washington, to a family with a rich history in business, politics, and community service. His great-grandfather had been a state legislator and mayor, his grandfather was the vice president of a national bank, and his father was a prominent and very wealthy lawyer.

Because young Bill excelled from his earliest school days, especially in science and math, his parents saw that he was enrolled in prestigious Lakeside Prep, known for its intense academic environment. This was in the late 1960s, when the world of computing was just beginning to peek over the horizon and carried a golden price tag. But no problem. To assure Lakeside's students wouldn't be left behind, the school held a fund-raiser and, with the proceeds, rented what it thought would be a year's worth of time on a computer owned by General Electric.

Bill Gates, his close friend Paul Allen, and a few others torpedoed that plan in a big hurry. They started hanging out in the computer room day and night, learning everything they could, even to the detriment of their other academic obligations. Within a matter of weeks, the expected year's worth of allotted computer time was gone, but that was no problem either. The school simply struck a new deal, this one with Seattle-based Computer Center Corporation, to get additional computer time at good rates.

That might have worked if young Gates and his friends hadn't immediately started (a) hacking into CCC's security system so they could reset the meter that tracked computer use and (b) crashing the system just for fun. They were caught, and the company banned Gates and his cohorts from its computers for several weeks. (The thought of Gates and Allen as the godfathers of a hacking subculture that has cost Microsoft and the world overall hundreds of billions of dollars does indeed boggle the mind.) But again, the exile was only temporary.

CCC's business was beginning to suffer from the system's weak security and the frequency with which it crashed—many of the same flaws Gates and his friends had been exploiting— so the company offered the gang a deal: find the bugs and pinpoint the weaknesses in the system, and they could have *unlimited* use of the computer.

In 1970, Computer Center Corporation ran into financial trouble that would eventually put it out of business, but by then, Gates and Allen had found a new computer home at the University of Washington, where Allen's father worked. Lakeside also pitched in: during Gates's junior year at the prep school, the administration offered him a job computerizing the scheduling system. Over the summer, Gates and Allen wrote the program, which coincidentally assured that Gates was assigned to classes with mostly girls—a sequence straight out of a nerd's revenge movie.

In the fall of 1973, Gates left Seattle to begin his freshman year at Harvard, part of his preprogrammed life plan. Allen, who almost certainly could have been admitted to Harvard along with his pal, chose a different route. He wanted hands-on experience, but the two remained in close contact, often discussing the potential of one day starting a company, and at the end of Gates's first year at Harvard, Allen moved closer to Boston so they could continue to pursue the still-vague possibilities. Then, in December of Gates's sophomore year, the vague future began to take on a more exact face.

On a visit to Harvard, Allen stopped at a convenience store and noticed the current issue of *Popular Electronics* magazine. On the cover, under the title "World's First Microcomputer Kit to Rival Commercial Models," was a picture of the Altair 8800. Energized as he had never been, Allen showed the magazine to Gates, and within a few days Gates had called the maker of the computer, Micro Instrumentation Telemetry Systems (MITS), and told them that he had written a BASIC computer program that could be used on the Altair.

This was a lie. Gates and Allen were just trying to gauge interest from the company. But MITS was deep in its own deception: the computer shown on the cover had not been developed yet, and even the prototype had been lost in shipping. Still, the magazine article had generated interest far exceeding expectations, so MITS asked Gates and Allen to come in and demonstrate what they were thinking. Only then did the two set out to write the code. Gates focused on programming while Allen worked on simulating how it would work on an Altair 8800, which they didn't have.

At the meeting eight weeks later, the program worked perfectly, and MITS arranged a deal to purchase the rights to Gates's BASIC. Gates would later say that it was at this moment he knew the software market had been born. Yet, despite his growing certainty of the opportunity in front of him, Bill Gates waited another 12 months, until his junior year, to drop out of school and, with Allen, form Micro-Soft. And even then, the company might have amounted to little more than a footnote in the history of software without Bill Gates's mother.

Long active in community service in the Seattle area, Mary Maxwell Gates became the first female president of the United Way of King County and eventually chair of the executive committee of the national United Way, then one of the most influential nonprofit positions in the world. Serving on the exec committee with her back in the early seventies were, among others, John Akers, who would later become the CEO and chairman of International Business Machines (IBM), and John Opel, who preceded Akers in both positions.

Mary Gates mentioned her son's new business to Opel, who by many accounts then relayed this information to other top IBM executives. There's no definitive record of what got said when to whom, but only a few weeks after Mary Gates got the ball rolling, IBM took a huge chance by contracting with Bill Gates's fledgling company to develop an operating system for the company's first personal computer. The success of both the IBM PC and the Microsoft Disc Operating System (or MS-DOS)—and the sweetheart deal that let Microsoft retain rights to its software—is what ultimately made Bill Gates the richest man on the planet.

Experience, Not Faith

So, did Bill Gates walk away from one of the world's most coveted degrees toward an uncertain path? Well, he did ultimately make decisions from which there would be no turning back. That part of the myth is dead on. But was Gates a great risk taker? That's a more complicated story.

His family's money and position provided cover for his youthful computing hijinks and helped assure that he would have the best education available. As for the famous Harvard dropout story, he didn't really. Rather, he took a formal "leave of absence," a kind of emotional umbilical cord that kept him tied to Harvard long after he had vacated the campus, just in case things didn't work out. But by then, he had already turned the odds in his favor. After half a decade of dancing with the opportunity, beginning early in high school, he had already covered most of his downside risks. He knew, for example, that he loved the work, and the early Micro-Soft had projects in the pipeline.

What's more, Gates had validation that both he and Allen were highly competent with this new technology, and he could see that the topside potential was huge. The industry was just emerging, and his mother was in the particularly influential position of head of a United Way executive committee that also included two future CEOs of the world's dominant computer company. As they say, it's often not what you know but who your mother knows that can land you billion-dollar contracts.

Far from being one of the world's great risk takers, Bill Gates might more accurately be thought of as one of the world's greatest risk *mitigators*. And in that, he is not alone.

The simple fact is that everyone is afraid of risk at some level, including everyone I interviewed for this book. That's a given of human nature. But the further fact is that Door No. 3 is a myth, whether we're talking about the myth of Bill Gates or the myths that we privately tell ourselves.

You don't *have* to be fearless to make dramatic changes in your life. Transformative change isn't propelled by raw courage. It's "sparked" by a series of events that build exposure and experience, both of which help to create asymmetric risk. Through sparking, the upside opportunity is confirmed while downside risk is mitigated. Ultimately, the leap—when it comes—is not one of faith but of experience, even of comfort, just as it was for Gates.

Knowing Before *Choosing*

When I was an executive recruiter, I was constantly dumbfounded by the decision-making process of the candidates I interviewed. I would make each potential job sound as glamorous and exciting as possible. But my scant initial presentation—usually not more than a few paragraphs—showed mostly what prospective employees would *be*, not what they would *do*: they would have this title, manage these people, live in this town, make this much money. More often than not, that's all people wanted to know. They rarely did deep research into the companies they were considering or asked themselves whether they would be good at the job or even like it. They would see a title (vice president) or a compensation figure ($150,000 per annum) and, for them, that would be all the bliss they thought they needed. They weren't taking leaps so much as they were running off a cliff and hoping someone had strung a net below.

The leap I'm writing about here is precisely the opposite. It's about knowing *before* you choose; it's about making certain the risk-return equation is leaning heavily in your favor. One of the ways you do that is by breaking down risk into its component parts and considering each one separately.

In fact, there are four distinct types of risk that impinge on any great life decision: passion risk (will I love it?), competency risk (will I be good at it?), opportunity risk (is there a real chance to succeed, a real market for what I want to sell?), and life-change risk (once I pass the point of no return, will I be better off?).

Most people spend the majority of their time in any leap decision process concentrating on the last of those risks—life-change—and leave the rest (passion, competency, opportunity) almost entirely up to chance. They believe that to make a leap is to open your eyes only *after* you have resolutely chosen Door No. 3. Only when you're on the other side do you learn if you have won a new car or an old goat. No wonder the Now Trap closes in around us so frequently when we contemplate great change in this way—the thought of laying everything on the table for an uncertain reward scares us into inaction.

Indeed, this is exactly what the Bill Gates myth is all about. But that's the myth. What Gates actually did—and what you can do, too—was to break down risk into its separate parts and tackle each one individually. He informed himself about the opportunity and test-drove the work to understand his passions and competencies, and only then did he make the formal commitment that would change his life direction. In short, he *educated* himself, *experimented* with the future, and only then leapt to *experience* it. Such is the cadence of the Spark Sequence, and the key to the leap itself.

Modeling the Future

In their book *Influencer: The Power to Change Anything*, authors Kerry Patterson, Joseph Grenny, David Maxfield, Ron McMillan, and Al Switzler tell the story of psychologist Albert Bandura's work with snake phobics. A much-praised Stanford University professor and former president of the American Psychological Association, Bandura and his assistants used newspaper ads to recruit men and women who were not just afraid of snakes, but who were seriously debilitated by their fear.

The goal of the experiment, Bandura told the subjects, was to make them so comfortable with snakes that they would be able to sit, unfazed, with a six-foot boa constrictor draped across their laps. To get them there, he had the phobics watch a man in the next room (a paid actor, although that was unknown to the subjects) as he supposedly tried to get over his own fears. The man would approach the boa, back away, approach a little closer, and so on, time and again, until finally he sat with the boa across his own lap.

Bandura then invited the subjects one by one to walk into the room and handle the boa themselves. Miraculously, simply watching the actor overcome his perceived fear of snakes was enough for some of the phobics to overcome their own fear. But most could not, and so they were given gloves, helmets, and other protective gear before they entered the room. Gradually, their fears ebbed, too, and within three hours, all the subjects were able to touch the snake without any protection and let it drape itself across their laps. One woman, who like many of the subjects had been plagued by snake-infested nightmares, actually dreamed shortly thereafter that a friendly serpent helped her wash the dishes.

For Bandura, this "guided mastery" is proof of the power of modeling to affect change not only in the short term but over a lifetime, and indeed, his work speaks forcefully to the value of mentors in any significant career shift. Not only do mentors model the future we aspire to, they also allow us to test our fears against their experience, and often they provide early buy-in once we do let go of the past. All that is invaluable.

To me, Bandura's snake phobics experiment also is a near-perfect textbook illustration of the Sparking Sequence at work. Some of the subjects sparked quickly and were done with their fear. Others sparked more slowly and deliberately. Some needed virtual full body armor before they could allow the boa near them. But all of them had first opened themselves up to the possibility that they could overcome their fear simply by responding to the ad. Then they were *educated* by the actor modeling the behavior. Next, they safely *experimented*, comforted by whatever protective gear they felt they needed. And finally, they brought themselves to *experience* the snake sitting on their laps. By facing down their phobias piece by piece, they were able finally to handle the boa unprotected.

Had the actor not modeled sparking for them, they never would have closed the gap between pessimism and optimism— between a past that had been defined by their phobia and a future they hoped would be free of it. Had they not been provided with protective gear and allowed to safely experiment with the notion, most would have been unable to gain the confidence firsthand that it could be done. And had they not done that, they would still be terrified of snakes to this day. Through his modeling, the actor both educated the subjects of the experiment and comforted them with the thought that they, too, could survive it. And the psychiatrist created a safe environment for them to test their fears in. From there, the phobics found their own individual ways to go through the experience.

That's what the sparking process does. It gives us time and space to educate ourselves, to do research, to seek out models and mentors. Then it provides a safe way for us to discover our passions and talents (or lack thereof) for a new direction. Maybe, like some of Bandura's subjects, we are ready to walk into the next room, or maybe we're not. But the point is that because we've kept our options open, we don't *have* to take the next step until we are convinced the risks have been sufficiently mitigated and that success is all but assured.

NASA, in its own way, does much the same thing with its astronauts. Anyone who has witnessed a space launch at Cape Canaveral close up knows what a simultaneously awesome and terrifying experience it is. A mile away across a lagoon, where the closest non-NASA spectators are generally allowed, the air pulsates with a physical intensity that leaves you feeling almost pummeled. In front of you, in the lagoon, the fish are jumping and thrashing madly. Over at the launchpad, the first moments of ascent seem maddeningly slow, and then, all of a sudden, what looks like a ball of fire begins to soar into the sky and, even on the clearest day or during the rare night launches, is soon out of sight.

How does NASA train astronauts not to be paralyzed by fear in those first moments of liftoff? Through this same combination of education and modeling. In Tom Wolfe's memorable phrase, the seven original Apollo astronauts had "the right stuff," and that culture continues to live within NASA. But more directly, NASA does it through training and simulations. All astronauts must complete an intensive two-year academic program at the Johnson Space Center, studying shuttle systems, meteorology, navigation, oceanography, and of course astronomy. Then they simulate different experiences, spending time in a microgravity-controlled water tank and taking flights in the "vomit comet," a modified jet that gives the feeling of weightlessness. Perhaps most important, they spend countless hours in a flight simulator, practicing every scenario imagin-

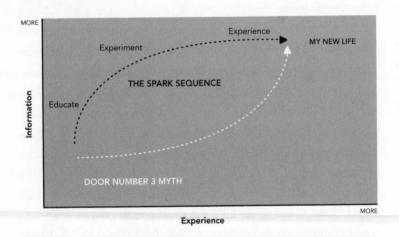

SPARK SEQUENCE

The Spark Sequence mitigates risk by allowing you to first educate yourself, then to safely experiment with the new direction, leaping only after the odds are sufficiently stacked in your favor. The Myth of Door Number 3 is the misbelief that you must first dive blindly and irreversibly in a new direction, rolling the dice on what you might find on the other side.

able. Without having been there, no one can know for certain what it's like to be at the tip of a flaming spear hurtling into deep space, but astronaut training simulates and replicates every possible situation over and over again so that a flight crew at the moment of liftoff will feel a sense of repetition as much as a sense of novelty.

Like Bandura's snake phobics, the NASA astronauts gathered information. They built exposure to what waited ahead and absorbed the trial experiences. Through hands-on experimentation, they tested the environment. They found their own premonitions of success. And finally, they acted.

Knowing by Doing

You can do the same in exploring and pursuing new directions for your career and life, and you don't have to junk your job or start a new company to get there. Educating yourself is the easiest part. Brad Margus stayed up late into the night reading medical journals to inform himself about his sons' illness. But this self-education stirred a new pool of questions, and ultimately set him on a path that would change his life direction forever.

When the idea hit me to attempt to write my first book, I hadn't a clue about what it might take to get published and quickly found that almost all of my preconceptions were inaccurate. But the point is just how quickly I found it out. Once you set the education process into motion, it is amazing how much information is out there and how accessible it really is.

There are equally as many ways to safely gain new trial experiences, and this trial exposure is critical. We've built an entire subculture around virtual experience, but the virtual will never substitute for the real. Without actually *doing*, you can never fully test your passion for or competency at whatever your future might hold.

Not long ago, I was at a conference where Tod Machover, the composer and music innovator, addressed this subject. "For decades," he said, "we have believed that if you play classical music to your babies while they are still in the womb, their IQs will jump 10 to 20 points. This is an exciting notion. Unfortunately, we now know that it doesn't work. The key for brain development, it turns out, is that you can't just listen to the music—you must *play* it."

So it is with the leap. You can't just read about it. You can't only dream about what life will be like on the other side if you ever want to really get there. GE's legendary boss Jack Welch put it very succinctly for me: "The best predictor of grades is grades."

Fear, quite simply, is the apprehension of the possibility of danger. To eliminate fear, we must fully understand possibility (that is, what the odds are) and equally understand what the danger is and what the utility of overcoming that fear will be in our life. Experience—doing—allows us to visualize the future and predict where we will be in it, and visualizing and predicting the future allows us to get there.

So, how do you experience without leaping? Well, volunteering lets you test your competency, whether it's volunteering away from your job in the off-hours or volunteering to take on new responsibilities at your workplace. Mentors within and outside your business can help you puzzle out opportunity risk even as they model the skills you will need to succeed. Volunteering and mentors, even a part-time job, can also help you test your passion against the real-world consequences of whatever you are contemplating, and testing passion can actually give you a premonition of success.

As I've stressed throughout this book, getting unstuck from whatever Now Trap has you in its grip doesn't require crashing through brick walls. It's not an all-or-nothing jump to something new. Rather, it's a matter of simultaneously building information and experience; of using mentoring, modeling, volunteering, and perhaps part-time work to educate yourself and to build exposure to whatever you are pointing toward.

Like artillery calibration, the leap is built on trial and error. A gunnery officer fires at a target, gets feedback on how much he missed by and in what direction, and then adjusts his weapon for the many variables that can affect accuracy. And then he keeps refiring and recalibrating until he hits the target dead-on.

So it is with the Spark Sequence. You're not counting on one shell to do the job. Rather, you are surrounding the issues as you search for the trajectory that will carry you to your ultimate life-change target. That makes all the difference.

In the end, you actually do have to sit atop a rocket exploding out of the earth's gravitational pull to know what the experience is really like. You must let that snake rest on your lap to know for certain that the phobia is gone. You must *do* it. You have to actually make the leap, but sparking lays the groundwork for that. It gives you time and space to gather information and experience so that in the end, when you do make the leap, you have confidence you are jumping to the right place.

One Foot in the Past, One in the Future

At the simplest level, everyone I interviewed for this book had the same story to tell. They all did a dual dance as they proceeded toward their leaps. They all kept one foot pointing toward the past while another stepped cautiously into the future. For as long as it took to launch their new trajectories, their lives were a series of endless adjustments through which they tested information, built exposure, found opportunity, and mitigated the risks involved.

Andy Levine and Brad Margus got to their leaps quickly. Andy was already plugged into the music industry. For him, the Rock Boat was a walk across the room. Brad had the urgency of his sons' medical condition pushing him forward. His passion was a given, and shrimp farming had honed his business sense. He learned on the fly because he had to. But speed is not the issue. What matters is that you provide time and space for the tension between what you have been and what you will be to work itself out.

During the years Jeff Gray was transitioning from a consultant to a full-time advocate for Atlanta's down-and-out, he lived like one of those dual-identity comic book superheroes: speeding through the inner-city streets at night to help battered drug addicts and hopping jets by day to close big business deals on the other side of the continent. Jeff says there was no question about which part of his dual existence brought him the greatest satisfaction. Practically from the moment he walked into that mission church, he felt as if he had come home. Yet Jeff clung to his past so tenaciously that he had to be told by his old clients that he had landed on the other side.

Sara Blakely is in some ways an even more powerful example of the gravitational pull of the status quo. Sara, you may recall, had completely visualized a different life for herself. She *knew* someday she would invent a product that would lead to self-employment and significant wealth. At the moment she cut the feet off her panty hose, she was convinced her vision had come true. Still, the external resistance and the built-in reluctance of the brain to accept a new direction wouldn't leave her alone.

"I kept hearing no, no no," she says, "and I would second-guess myself. One day I was so mentally confused by it, I said, 'Enough, I'm letting it go. I'm either supposed to do this or not supposed to. Give me a sign either way.'

"A couple of weeks later I was doing a sales seminar for Danka in Detroit. Afterward, I went to my hotel room and turned on the last few minutes of *Oprah*, just as she lifted her pant leg to show that she had solved a garment problem by cutting the feet off her panty hose. 'Okay,' I said, 'that's the sign. That's it.' "

Yet even then—even with the stars aligned, Oprah spreading omens, and her own chutzpah to burn—Sara hadn't sufficiently mitigated the risks in her own mind to let go of what she had been.

"I didn't quit my job at Danka until after I had landed Neiman Marcus and Saks Fifth Avenue," she says. "I had a prototype, production capability, and two customers, and only then did I finally take the leap."

And what a leap it was. A short time later, Sara was sitting in her apartment when an *Oprah* staffer called to say that the SPANX feetless panty hose would soon air on the show as one of Oprah Winfrey's favorite things. Another five years later, to bring her story full circle, Sara gave Oprah a surprise present: a million-dollar check for her charity. Thus a leap becomes almost a fairy tale, but in this case a staggeringly true one.

Looking back, I can now see that my own life transition amounted to a series of explorations into new areas with little or no risk. I was moving forward—there's no question about that—but in each case, before I made a concrete step in a new direction, I had already mitigated the change danger while keeping my existing trajectory options open for as long as possible. In the end, I wasn't really giving anything up in making the change. In fact, by then I had discovered that my biggest risk would be not to pursue it.

Finding the Future That Is Right for You

Why spark? Why go through it all? Why bother with this dual dance? The answer once more goes back to your own personal evolution. No matter what your current station in life, happiness and fulfillment will remain only if you continue to change and grow in a direction unique to you, and on your own terms. The Spark Sequence helps us build experience so that we can choose the safest or most accurate or quickest or most mitigating path to get there, whatever our personal risk-aversion needs happen to be.

Consider the experience of Jeffrey Merrihue. Like many of the rest of us, Jeffrey found himself stuck on a career path not of his own making—in his case, at Kellogg's—doing work that brought him little pleasure.

"I was an ordinary food marketer struggling to break out of the double stereotype of 'food' and 'marketing'," he says. "For years, I had been focused on only one thing—selling Oreos or selling Corn Flakes. That had lost its appeal long ago, so I did this subconscious review of my strengths and what really interested me, and I determined I needed to head in a different direction. I decided to go into services where I could deploy lots of ideas across lots of clients.

"A colleague and I had created some really interesting analytics at Kellogg's, and we thought we might be able to commercialize them. Basically, the idea was to apply financial analysis to marketing data and then present it in a simple fashion. The immediately relevant industry sector wasn't big, but we still thought this was a great idea, and we were fairly certain we had the competency between us to pull it off. But unfortunately, we chose the wrong path to get there: joining a faltering media agency.

"Eighteen months later, my colleague and I realized that our very good idea was being bogged down by this struggling company in a struggling industry. The sensible thing to do at that point would have been to give up and go back into food marketing. We both *knew* we could do that. But what on paper might have looked like a career misstep was actually an invaluable experience. It taught us both a lot about our idea and ourselves. In our own terms, we both concluded that we would rather barely survive doing something cutting-edge than get comfortable again doing pretty much rote work.

"So we tried again, this time at Accenture, a great company in a great industry. And in only five years, we went on to create a $150-million sector from scratch."

In all, 24 months passed between the day Jeffrey and his colleague began to launch their leap by leaving Kellogg's and the time they finally landed at Accenture and things began to visibly take off. Two years is a long span in any career, but it wasn't a time-out. Their sparking confirmed their passion; it built faith in their competency; it let them try out venues where their idea might blossom; and finally, it brought them to the one venue where passion and competency could blossom forth to the tune of $150 million annually.

That's what sparking does. It gives us space to try on futures until we find the one that is just right for us. The poet John Keats referred to all this as "negative capability"—"the ability to be in mystery and doubt without irritable searching after fact and reason"—and praised Shakespeare for having it in abundance. Others have called it less erudite things. The point is that the more variants you put out and the more you let them find their own way and level, the more you will be prepared for whatever comes your way.

"You put multiple irons in the fire and fate will show you where to direct your attention" is how Sara Blakely puts it today.

As Much Sparking as It Takes

You might recall my colleague who wanted to transition from head-hunting to writing but couldn't take the leap until he had numerous articles accepted for publication. Another writer friend took far more sparking than that.

"Ever since I was in college," he explains, "I'd had a vision of myself writing books and living in an old place in the country with my wife and dog. But by the early 1990s I had been in journalism for more than 20 years and hadn't had anything published that was longer than a magazine article.

"Then a literary agent I had contacted on some other matter called me with a proposition. A publisher she knew wanted a biography of one of the heroes of the first Gulf War. The advance would be minimal and the work had to be done in a hurry. In fact, the publisher wanted the manuscript done, from scratch, in five months. Was I interested?

"Well, I figured this was my chance to find out if I really liked working at that length, so I said sure. Over the next two months, I did 125 interviews before and after work, during lunch, on weekends, whenever I could find the time. I convinced my boss to let me take a three-month leave of absence, which gobbled up every penny of the advance. I chained myself to the keyboard and wrote. And in the end I think the book surprised both my publisher and me. It got some very good reviews and sold a decent number of copies in hardback and in paper, but the real point is that I loved, and I mean *loved*, writing it."

With his passion risk satisfied, my friend next tackled competency.

"There's no question that writing the biography rekindled my old dream, but I had no way of knowing if the book had been a one-hit wonder, and with two kids, the oldest in college, I couldn't afford to take huge chances. So I contacted an agent I vaguely knew and told him that I would be glad to ghost-write books and rescue manuscripts as well as write them. A month later he sent me a box stuffed with 472 single-spaced pages of a manuscript that was so tangled up it was hard to find the beginning and the end. I unsnarled that and came up with a proposal, and that led to a multibook deal, so I knew I had two marketable skills to support me."

Satisfying his competency risk inevitably led my friend to

confront his opportunity risk, although he never would have used the phrase.

"The fact is, I was one of the top three people at the magazine where I was working. It depended on how you read the masthead. That gave me a certain importance, and it wasn't that I despised what I was doing. Most days I was fairly content, but I kept having the feeling that instead of being content, I could be happy.

"I was trying to figure out what to do when another book came my way, a companion volume to a TV documentary. I wrote that, and then I edited and half-ghosted two or maybe three more books, one of which ended up a *New York Times* best seller. And by the time all that was through, I knew I could succeed, not just financially but on my terms. And that left only one more problem: I was getting ready to jump ship and swim to an island. Was I really going to like the island once I got there? That mattered a lot to me because I knew that once I left journalism, I never wanted to come crawling back."

And thus my author-friend confronted the last and culminating risk: life-change.

"Although I had been working at home in fits and starts, I didn't know what it was going to be like to wake up every Monday morning for the rest of my working life and have nowhere to go except downstairs to my office. So I made my editor in chief an offer: I would voluntarily reduce my pay by 60 percent if he would reduce my workweek by 40 percent, with Mondays and Fridays free.

"If ever there was a win-win situation, this was it. He got my experience at a deep discount. For my part, I knew the outside work would probably more than pay for the lost salary, and I figured this way I would get to know for sure if I was the person I had been dreaming about for so long. Two years later, I quit the job for good—that was no longer me working there. And five years after that, my wife and I moved to a 215-year-old house in the Virginia countryside. The dog is on hold, but that's about all.

"It took me seven years to disengage myself from the past, and twelve years to walk into the old dream. And I don't have a moment's regret."

My friend sat there quietly for a moment, as if reliving all the sparking that had finally set him off on his new life's trajectory. Then he nodded his head, walked over to his bookshelves, and rummaged through a photo album until he came across the shot he wanted: it showed a gleeful, chubby three-year-old suspended in midair, halfway between the side of the swimming pool and the waiting arms of his father (my friend, 25 years younger), who was standing up to his waist in the water.

"That's it!" he said, triumphant.

"What's it?" I asked.

"Everything I just described. Take a close look. We all appear happy as larks, don't we? But it was cold in that water, and I had been waiting there for fifteen minutes while my son walked up to the edge, looked at the water and at me with my arms out, got ready to jump, then backed away again and thought about it some more.

"He was already comfortable in the water. My wife had put him through one of those water-babies courses when he was only a year old. The kid was a fish. But this was something new, and he had to account for all those possible dangers before he acted:.'Do I really want to do jump? Will I be good at it? Is my dad going to pull his arms away at the last minute?' Not until he had decided in his own mind that all those risks were sufficiently accounted for to be worth the reward of jumping into the pool on his own could he bring himself to do it, and by midair, he was already so happy he couldn't stand it.

"Human nature doesn't change much, does it?"

Answering the Questions
That Hold Us Back

In fact, human nature doesn't change dramatically over most lifetimes. The stage gets bigger. The stakes mount higher. Variance enters in. Some kids go charging off the side of the pool into the water with barely a second thought and continue doing so throughout life. Others linger on the pool's edge, real and metaphorical, for what seems an eternity. But we're all slip-sliding somewhere along the risk-mitigation scale from the first step we take to nearly the final one.

Whatever our personal risk quotient, the simple fact is that we can't change until we mitigate the fears that hold us back, and we can't mitigate those fears simply by analyzing our way around them. Not only is the pull of the present too strong, we also are hardwired to imagine the future in accord with the present. To return to Albert Bandura and his snake phobics, it wasn't that they didn't want to be cured of their terror. They wanted nothing more. They just couldn't envision a world in which that terror wouldn't exist. Bandura got them over the hump by having an actor model conquering the fear and then providing a safe environment for them to gain the experience that allowed the desired outcome to take place.

As with Bandura's snake phobics, so it goes with the rest

of us. Sparking lets us answer the questions that hold us back. Answering those questions enables us to believe. Once we believe, we can act. And—the miracle of the whole process— once we act, so many of our fears and perceived risks fall right away because of the real truth our brain doesn't want us to let us in on: it wants out of the Now Trap it has created. The brain *wants* us to be free to change. It knows the difference between a stagnant pond and a free-flowing spring.

Our Primary Color points us to the door that is right for us alone. Big, selfless, and simple ideas bear us along in our quest. And the Spark Sequence is the abracadabra that throws open the gates to the future and narrows the chasm in front of us so that we need only a small and inevitable step to reach already-known terrain.

And thus we have arrived at our last and most critical set of questions: in what direction should I now be headed, and on whose terms?

My Leap Journal—
The Spark Sequence

Describe a bold dream for your life, one that almost seems
overly ambitious. Write down five to ten questions that, if
you knew their answers, would dramatically reduce the
uncertainty about this aspiration. Which of these questions
can be answered through research? Through discussions
with mentors or others?

What trial experiences can I gain that may shed additional
light and build confidence toward this new potential path?

What is stopping me from beginning to crack open the door?

Aristotle on a Lily Pad: A Perspective on Life-Work Design

8

In 1896, without much enthusiasm, a small team of academics and students began excavating an ancient landfill just outside the town of Oxyrhynchus, 100 miles south-southwest of modern Cairo. Oxyrhynchus (the name comes from a Nile fish famous in Egyptian mythology for eating the penis of Osiris) was thought to have little real promise as an archeological site, and the initial finds seemed to confirm that.

Then, two Oxford University undergrads stumbled upon a vast archive of blackened papyrus, the predecessor of modern paper, made from reeds that grew along the Nile. Oxyrhynchus, it turned out, had flourished under Greek rule several centuries before Christ and continued to prosper into the Roman era, and the Oxyrhynchus Papyri, as the discovery came to be known, were a breathtaking assortment of classical manuscripts, the largest collection of them ever discovered.

One of the archeologists would later recall that "[m]erely

turning up the soil with one's boot would frequently disclose a layer." Included among the documents were whole or partial works by the playwrights Aristophanes and Sophocles and the poet Sappho, fragments of the Gospels, and accounts of daily life in the Greco-Roman empire 2,000 years earlier.

Climate and topography preserved the documents— Oxyrhynchus had been located on a canal, not the Nile itself, and so was out of the river's floodplain. And sand sealed them off for the most part from the worst effects of exposure to the atmosphere. But reading the vast bulk of them proved almost impossible.

The papyri were fragile and fragmentary, worm-eaten, dirty, and so blackened by the passage of time that they were almost entirely illegible. Inevitably, the elation of discovery succumbed to the mind-numbingly slow pace of translation. Generations of scholars have slaved over the task but so far have managed to render intelligible to any degree only about 5,000 of the estimated 500,000 fragments found. Sitting stacked in nearly 800 boxes at Oxford University, these documents have caused excitement and frustration in equal measure for more than a century.

In early April 2005, however, a team of scientists led by Dirk Obbink, an American-born scholar now teaching at Oxford, made a startling discovery. By using a digital camera with a series of ultraviolet and infrared filters, they could highlight as never before the contrasts between text and background in manuscripts that had been previously undecipherable. More than a century after this treasure chest of ancient documents was first located, we are finally beginning to truly open it.

One of the grandest discoveries thus far in this newly

readable cache of the Oxyrhynchus Papyri has been sections of Aristotle's lost book *Invitation to Philosophy*. The son of the court physician to the king of Macedonia and a student of Plato, Aristotle was one of the leading thinkers of the ancient world. For more than a thousand years, his *Invitation* had inspired readers to a more philosophical approach to life. Then, sometime in the murk of the Dark and Middle Ages, this vital book all but disappeared, reduced to a few scattered reports and echoes in other texts. Now, thanks to Obbink and his team, one of the seminal voices and intellects in the entire history of civilization has been brought back to life.

So what does Aristotle have to say from his ancient pedestal that is useful and relevant to us today? A great deal, it turns out. In the restored manuscripts, he draws a critical distinction between outcomes caused by skill or intellect and those caused by chance or luck. Even when two outcomes are identical, Aristotle argues, those that result from deliberate action have much greater value than those that occur willy-nilly, without any particular intent on our part.

Imagine, by way of illustration, two sailors starting out from the same dock. One tacks left and right, riding the wind and playing the tides and current as best he can. The other quickly tires of all that, furls his sail, naps on the deck, and lets the boat drift where it will. Conceivably, both could end up several hours later at the same point. It might even be a pleasant place to arrive at, but Aristotle would argue that the end point, in fact, has utterly different meaning for the two sailors because the journeys that got them there are nothing alike.

For an outcome to truly matter, for it to have deep value to our lives, we have to be in control of the actions that get us there. We have to be the one steering the ship—the one deciding which way to tack and when, and how much reach to give the sails. If we simply let ourselves drift toward happiness or fulfillment or any other goal—or if we let others determine the route that will get us there or what the goal itself will be—we have lost control of our own journey and can never fully enjoy or even, at a subconscious level, embrace the outcome.

Self-Determination (Emphasis on Self)

Aristotle would have understood perfectly the concept of the subconscious—he wrote a treatise on dreams. But the concept of *career* would have been foreign to him. In Periclean Athens, a man of great talent would answer many summonses over the course of a lifetime: he served the state and the arts; he improved learning and culture. Still, what Aristotle has to say in his *Invitation to Philosophy* is as applicable to a modern work life as it was to any calling in his own time. The more we let external forces determine the work we do and the success we achieve, the more we discount the outcome and see the world through other people's eyes. A career has maximum meaning and purpose in direct proportion to the self-determination we put into it.

Anne Lamott writes about this in a slightly different context in her memoir *Bird by Bird*. In the course of teaching writing to hundreds of students, Lamott recounts, she has noticed a recurring pattern: all her students want to be published, but many don't want to write.

"You'll never get to where you want to be that way, I tell them. There is a door we all want to walk through, and writing can help you find it and open it. Writing can give you what having a baby can give you: It can get you to start paying attention, can help you soften, can wake you up. But publishing won't do any of those things; you'll never get it that way."

So it is with many other endeavors. We look to the end result without considering the journey that will get us there. We cherish the outcome but discount the process and experience that will make it possible.

We want to be a movie star without contemplating 15-hour workdays or the misery of casting calls; we long to own an idyllic bed-and-breakfast but have never been a host; we dream of being a corporate VP but have never stopped to truly consider all the lost days with our loved ones that getting there will entail. I'm as guilty as the next person. I took up the guitar in high school because I believed that guys who play guitars have better luck attracting girls and I desperately wanted to be able to do that. The trouble was, I found the tedious hours of practice an utterly ridiculous requirement to get there. If I had spent more time practicing and less time visualizing myself onstage with David Cassidy, it might have actually worked.

As I wrote earlier, the Spark Sequence provides us time and space to make sure our passions are earnest and the opportunities before us real. Sparking gives us a chance to test our dreams, and more than one of them. But, finally, if you are not willing to embrace and celebrate the path—to dive beneath the dream to what will truly get you there—the outcome, whatever it is, will never be as meaningful as it could and should be.

Simply put, it's the journey that counts, not whatever trappings of success might lie at the end. It's how we get there that builds meaning in the outcome and makes certain we're progressing toward our own best destiny, not borrowing someone else's.

Value for What? For Whom?

Not long ago, I was watching my three children race around the house when four-year-old Arden stumbled upon a jar of jelly beans. The jar had been sitting in the same place for days but only now had caught her attention, and as it did, you could almost see the lightbulb go off in her head. Suddenly, Arden turned to her two siblings, three-year-old brother Adam and two-year old sister Laine, and began talking about how great jelly beans are and what a find this jar was. In fact, she said, it was *so* great a find that she might just be able to figure out a way that they could have some if . . .

The *if* seemed to do it. Within moments, Adam and Laine wanted nothing more than a taste of the jelly beans, so Arden made Adam pick up the clothes in her room for his first jelly bean, made Laine go get her a drink for the second one, and on and on. But Adam, it turned out, had very particular ideas about which jelly beans are best. In fact, he *always* chose a red one, and it wasn't many rounds of chores before nearly all the reds were gone.

Once Arden noticed the red jelly beans had been all but scraped up, the tide turned. Mind you, she still controlled an entire jar of jelly beans, but now all she wanted were the scarce red ones. Naturally, these being two-, three- and four-year-olds, a fight soon broke out that took nearly half an hour and an episode of *Barney* to calm down, but what was so fascinating to me was that once their attention was turned to something else, the jelly beans themselves lost all their value.

Arden initially had been able to set the perception of value very high even though the value was by any objective standard completely artificial. Without having a clue what he was really doing, Adam gained the upper hand by creating scarcity in a particular element of the asset class involved. In both instances, wants and needs were determined not intrinsically but from what others had.

Kids, right? All of us who have them have seen a drama like this played out before us, and we've probably all told ourselves they'll get over it as they grow up. But in fact, they—and we—for the most part never do. The stakes get bigger, the prizes higher, but so often we continue from cradle to grave to do just what Arden and Adam were doing in my living room: let others determine what's of greatest value to us and then base our needs not on what is best for us but on what other people have.

Here's another example of the Jelly Bean Fallacy, this from the opposite end of the earning spectrum:

Three decades ago, almost no one knew or much cared what a CEO was paid. Sure, it was more than the average Joe, but that was to be expected. The boss gets the biggest share of the pie. Then a series of very high-priced payouts caught the public's eye—and more important, the media's outrage—and prompted a variety of regulatory measures meant to bring executive pay out into the sunshine. Sheer embarrassment, it was thought, would solve the problem. But guess what happened once transparency ruled? CEO pay took off like a rocket.

To cite one prominent example, as late as 1993, when the compensation engine was just starting to barrel down the track, then–Exxon CEO Lawrence Rawls received total annual pay of slightly less than $3 million. A mere dozen years later, Rawls's successor as CEO, Lee Raymond, raked in over $70 million. To be sure, Exxon had become a more complicated enterprise in the interim between Rawls and Raymond, but was the company 23.3 times more difficult to oversee? That's hard to imagine.

How did the transparency movement turn so sour? It's simple actually. CEOs are humans, too. Once they could see along with the general public what their fellow CEO down the road was making, they needed that amount as well, plus just a *little* bit more. It didn't matter that they might be earning more annually than small foreign nations. Nor did it matter that an extra $1 million or $10 million had absolutely no marginal utility in their lives. In fact, what they earned didn't matter at all. What really mattered was what they *hadn't* been paid—whatever amount would have put them on top of the peer heap. Until they had that, someone else had all the red jelly beans. *Waaaah!*

In his study of behavioral economics, *Predictably Irrational*, MIT professor Dan Ariely cites the example of a gem dealer named James Assael. Back in the 1970s when he was traveling around the blue-lagoon paradises of French Polynesia, Assael stumbled on a Frenchman who told him that off the coast of his particular island was a rare variety of "black-lipped" oysters, from which came even more rare "black" pearls.

The two men soon went into business together, and Assael went to New York, hoping to create a market for these rare gems. He got nowhere with his marketing plan, though, and returned to Polynesia without having made a single sale or generating even a whisper of interest. The rare black pearls were evidently worthless. But Assael regrouped, and soon returned to New York with a new approach, convincing his buddy Harry Winston to display a string of black pearls in Winston's famous show window on Fifth Avenue in Manhattan, this time with a ridiculously high price tag. Suddenly everyone wanted what no one had cared about only days before, and a new and highly prosperous submarket of precious gems was born.

What has scarcity has value. We all know that—that's freshman economics, whether we're talking jelly beans or the last few dollars that will land us on top of the highest-paid heap or pearls basically the color of chimney soot. But value for what? For whom? That's the side of the equation we don't focus on.

Take a moment to write down on a clean sheet of paper the ten things you most love to do. Next to each, write down how many times in the last year you did them. On a second page, note all the things you bought within the last two years that were wants, not actual needs, and then calculate all the baggage that has come with those purchases: maintenance, time, complexity, not to mention extra hours at the office to pay them off.

If your "how many times" list is long and the baggage list minimal, congratulations. But odds are that as you look at your list, you'll see that you are filling your life up with stress over things that ultimately don't matter, to the sacrifice of rarely doing and being with the things and people you most love.

There's a wonderful Buddhist saying I came across recently that has a lot to do with the subject at hand: "Western culture is a very major response to a very minimal set of problems."

That's what is crazy about so many of our lives, not the fact that we strive. Striving is good. It gives the journey meaning. But too often we strive toward goals that don't fulfill us, goals that aren't in sync with our own inner lives. Like fast-food devotees, we load up on the empty calories of life and ignore the sustenance that satisfies anything other than our immediate hunger.

Why? Because we have been conditioned that way. Because we are taught how to succeed but almost never how to define success in personal terms. The difference is as broad as an ocean.

Think of it. From practically the beginning of our cognitive lives, we are judged by a series of linear "success" scales with well-defined positive and negative terminals, all of them pointing us in the same direction. On report cards, "A" is always better than "C" is always better than "F." Stanford outranks Florida State outranks Wayne State. MBA tops BA tops AA. The scales by which we adults measure ourselves are only extensions of the same ones by which we have been measured (and have measured ourselves) all along. A $200,000 salary is preferable to $100,000 is preferable to $50,000. CEO beats COO beats division head beats regional manager and on and on.

Individually, all these propositions are entirely defensible. If salary matters to you—and it does to just about everyone—who wouldn't prefer $200,000 annually to half or a quarter that much? If titles are important, why not shoot for CEO? That's where the career ladder is pointing.

The problem comes when we allow these linear bases of comparison to become the benchmarks of our own success and happiness without ever stopping to seriously consider what definition of "success" and "happiness" best suits each of us individually. When we do that, we're seeing the world through someone else's eyes, playing according to rules we haven't set, aspiring to goals that others have told us are the ones that count.

It doesn't matter whether we are talking about job titles or corner offices or larger houses or country clubs or the new cars with dashboard veneers hand-carved by Tibetan monks. So long as we allow those external to us set the "value" for any object or experience, it will always be "value" with as asterisk, like a Barry Bonds home-run record. And the more asterisks we have on our value chart, the more likely we are to end up with a fancy title sitting in the corner window office, wondering how we ever got duped into paying so much for all these jelly beans.

The Right Journey

Successfully orchestrating your own leap isn't about money or titles. It's not about founding a company or saving the world or, really, outcomes of any kind. Great outcomes happen when you get the rest of it right. The leap isn't even about happiness, although I know no one who has made the kind of leap I'm writing about who isn't a far more complete and content person today as a result.

The leap is about making certain you are on the right journey. It's about living in your own Primary Color, your own intersection of passions and strengths, and not trying to squeeze into someone else's intersection. It's about putting square pegs in square holes and round pegs in round holes and not trying to force ourselves into roles that were never meant for us, or slaving toward a prize we will ultimately discover is worth very little. In Aristotelian terms, it's about the meaning and value derived from intentionality, from being in control of your life's own direction. But at the very deepest level, the leap is about one more thing still: it's about finding the right lily pad.

What do I mean by that? Just this: the lily pad is the place from which we view the world, the perspective that tells us what it means to be successful and fulfilled in our careers.

I recently had a very interesting conversation with National Geographic explorer Wade Davis, who told me that he estimates that there are some 60,000 distinct human cultures in the world today. His life journey, he said, was to meet and live with a broad diversity of those cultures, including the most remote. The lesson from his decades of such explorations? That the world we live in does not exist in some absolute sense. We all sing and dance, but the melody of the song and the cadence of the dance is different all around the world.

As we spoke, I thought back to elementary school and being shown a brief video of a newly discovered primitive tribe in Africa, one that appeared not to have developed from our own ancestors thousands of years ago. How had they been so held back, I remember thinking back then? But now, talking with Wade, I could see that these different cultures aren't necessarily backward. They simply have other ways of thinking, other ways of being, other ways of orienting themselves to the world. These are not just less-successful imitations of Western culture, but rather 60,000 different interpretations of what it means to be alive and happy in this life.

Think of the world for a moment as a giant pond, and then

think of those 60,000 distinct cultures as lily pads filling the pond. Numbers like these are always loosey-goosey, but whatever number you agree with, multiply it by all the permutations and combinations within each of those distinct cultures, and clearly there's a lily pad for literally everyone in the world to call his or her home.

In theory, that should give us all a chance to view the ripples that spread out across the pond differently, to aspire to different goals, to define success and happiness in highly personal terms. In practice, though, we tend to all gather on the same lily pad with those in our peer group so that our goals and perspectives and the things that make us happy and sad are only marginally different, if at all, from those around us.

An example: Back in the 1990s, researchers set out to measure compensation and happiness among business school graduates from a decade earlier. Not surprisingly, Harvard MBAs were off the charts when it came to compensation. On average, they earned roughly twice the pay of any other business school's alumni ten years out. When it came to happiness, though, the Harvard grads weren't even in the top 20.

The study didn't pinpoint exactly why, but I think the answer is obvious. If Harvard MBAs had each developed individual definitions of happiness in accord with their passions and strengths, and if they had been working toward them, they couldn't possibly have been so collectively sad. In business, Harvard grads are the ones who hold Willy Wonka's Golden Ticket. The world is at their feet.

But they hadn't done that. Basically, these MBAs were viewing the world from the same lily pad. Happiness to them equaled a combination of material attainment and career advancement as measured only against their peer group. "A

Harvard MBA," an alumnus of the school once told me, "is a very hard thing to get over." No wonder they were unhappy. No wonder so many felt stuck in the Now Trap. Only one person can win that game, just as only one person can win the CEO game of who gets paid the most and the fashion game of who has the longest strand of the rarest black pearls in all the world. And even when you do win it, what have you won? A game whose rules were set by someone else in the first place. That's not winning. It's succumbing.

Variance, Not Stasis

Winning is trying and failing. Winning is finding your own lily pad, your own definition of success, your own rules of happiness. Winning, in a word, is *variance*, not conformity.

Aristotle knew this. That's why the journey is far more important than the outcome. Darwin knew it, too. Variance is absolutely central to his theory of evolution. And despite all its bitching and moaning about maintaining the status quo, our brain knows it as well.

When it is functioning at its best, the brain is constantly seeking out new connections and expanding its pathways. Gerontologists encourage the elderly to take up a new hobby—a musical instrument, painting, a foreign language—for this very reason: the brain wants these new connections. Its very nature is to be additive, not subtractive.

But the issue goes beyond that. Not only does the brain pursue change, it is constantly changed in the process. All of the data that come in from the external world—all of the thoughts that even fleetingly enter and leave our brains—permanently alter our perception of everything in the future, including how we evaluate any additional thoughts and experiences.

The same thing happens as we hop from lily pad to lily pad in search of a perspective that fits the intersection of our strengths and passions and as we spark our way from pathway to pathway, trying out different iterations of the person and life we are on the way to becoming. We might stay on the pad only for a moment; we might realize in a relative instant that we are on the wrong track, pursuing the wrong goal in the wrong way. But exposing ourselves even to the possibility of change in a particular direction permanently enriches our experience set and the lens through which we view our world.

Species advancement is predicated not on infallible consistency, but on the consistent failure of DNA strands to replicate properly. That failure produces genetic variations that allow species to survive when the struggle for life gets perilous, and the variations in turn become the new norm of the species until fresh crises require more failure and thus more variation and ultimate success.

It's the failure-proof variation-averse species that either perish or inhabit a kind of eternal biological status quo. In an online column for the *New York Times* Web site, the evolutionary biologist Olivia Judson tells the story of the remarkable bread mold *Neurospora crassa*. *Neurospora* is so averse to variation—and so intent on protecting its genome from invasion—that whenever a large segment of DNA gets duplicated, it bombards the copy with what are known as "point mutations" that effectively turn the genetic code into nonsense.

To be sure, the process works. Among bread molds, *Neurospora* is a virtual citadel, but hundreds of millions of years have gone by, and *Neurospora* is still, after all, only a bread mold. As Judson delicately puts it, "Its use of mutations to defend its genome from invasion may have inadvertently blocked off some evolutionary paths." If you have read this far, odds are strong that's *not* what you want for your work or your life.

Memes, Innovation, and the Curse of Competency

Species aren't alone in advancing through change and variation. Cultures advance in the same evolutionary way. Just as genetic traits compete within the genome for dominance, so ideas, ways of doing things, songs and stories, even words compete within any given culture for the upper hand. The ones that win out get copied and passed along, and the greater variance they can produce along the way, the better their chances of surviving from generation to generation and even millennium to millennium. As with genomes, civilizations with static cultures bog down in the march of time, while ones with dynamic, constantly evolving cultures charge forward.

One leading theorist of cultural evolution, the British academician Susan Blackmore, goes so far as to argue that it was cultural selection far more than genetic selection that caused the human brain to expand so dramatically in volume over the last two to three million years. The brain, she argues, grew because the need to successfully copy ways of doing and thinking about things and even remembering things forced it to grow to keep up with cultural imperatives.

There's a word for this emerging science of cultural evolution and selection: memetics, named for the "memes" or cultural units on which it is based. A meme can be as trivial as the way a maid in a five-star hotel folds the end of a roll of toilet paper or the way Silicon Valley executives dress casually for work. The point is, that the winning memes in the evolutionary battle for cultural superiority get copied and spread like wildfire, and soon every maid in every five-star hotel around the world, it seems, is folding toilet paper tips the same way, and every high-tech exec is donating his neckties to Goodwill.

Blackmore happens to be one of memetics' edgiest and most captivating proponents. I admire her for that, and I think her field of learning has much to teach us, but I sometimes prefer to think of the whole business as the madcap kitchen of a sprawling Italian restaurant. The stoves are full of pots, different kinds of pasta are bubbling away in each of them, and a crazed chef moves up and down the line, picking out individual zitis and rigatonis and elbow macaronis and slinging them against the wall. If they stick, the pasta is done. If not, it has longer to cook.

Which memes stick? Which units of knowledge triumph in this cultural warfare and which fall away? Well, we already know the answer to that. Big ideas get attention. Selfless ideas engage others in our cause. And simple ones are easy to replicate. But what's equally important—and what evolution teaches us time and again—is that variety matters, too. The more pots that are boiling on the stovetop and the more different kinds of pasta that are cooking in them, the better the chance you'll have just the right kind of pasta done to perfection at the moment you need it.

Companies prove the value of variation every day. In his book *Weird Ideas That Work*, Stanford professor Robert Sutton explored what makes a company innovative. He looked at process, culture, people, almost everything you can think of, and the only thing that correlated definitively with innovation was the *amount* of times a company tried. The ones that innovated the most, like 3M, were simply the ones who tried more.

People prove it, too, and even more convincingly. Those who continue to explore new paths, who hop from lily pad to lily pad in search of the right perspective, are the ones most likely to find the path that sweeps them to an extraordinary life. In an odd way, this is nature's little joke on excellence. In the personal evolutionary struggle for fulfillment, those of us with ordinary skills are in many ways the most advantaged.

Let me explain what I mean by that. Back when Jim Citrin and I were doing the research for *The 5 Patterns of Extraordinary Careers*, we noticed (but failed to adequately develop) two interesting phenomena. The first was that people who broke out of the crowd and did amazing things with their work lives were not mostly those who had been on a single career track straight out of high school but, rather, those who had explored numerous paths, a variety of roles, different industries, even living in different cities and sometimes nations.

The second related and equally unexplored phenomenon we labeled the Curse of Competency: just as following a path preordained from the teen years or earlier can have a stifling affect on a career, so too can very high levels of competency. Why? Because highly competent people tend to get routed early in life into specific fields—law, medicine, finance—where they are quickly promoted and richly rewarded.

All that's fine in the short term, but being routed into adult life, as opposed to finding their own route, means they never get a chance to discover their Primary Color, their own specific intersection of strengths and passions. That comes from knocking around and getting knocked around. It comes from failure as well as success. For the highly competent, the natural design processes of evolution—the ones that allow us to test out multiple variations on our future—have less chance to work. That's one large reason, I think, why so many materially successful doctors, lawyers, hedge-fund managers, and the like are often so fundamentally unfilled by their work lives.

Personal Evolution

I wrote at the beginning of this book that the leap is personal evolution. Allow me, then, in these closing pages to review just how that is so and how the whole idea of evolution—species, cultural, and personal—winds its way through the three elements of the leap process that I have been describing.

Like species and cultural development, personal evolution works best under conditions that most favor variation and change.

That's how you test out alternate definitions of yourself, how you find your Primary Color, how you land finally on the lily pad that is right for you.

As with species and cultural development, not all potential changes are equally advantaged.

In Darwinian terms, there are vast genetic variation possibilities, but only the "fittest" can survive. In memetics terms, the possible variations on cultural units will always exceed the capacity of even the most spacious brain to absorb and hold on to them. What gives a meme oomph, what puts a genetic change over the top, is its properties. Big, selfless, and simple will always win out over small, selfish, and complex.

Personal evolution is most likely to be successful under conditions in which small changes can produce very large potential results.

This also might seem counterintuitive. Don't huge results require huge undertakings? Empirically, though, we know what rot that is. Sara Blakely sent huge change rolling simply by applying for a patent. Brad Margus started his giant leap with a dime-store-size nonprofit. Simply trying to help the homeless person in front of him catapulted Jeff Gray into an amazing new life. In fact, these were all extremely minor changes in life direction, yet each led to major changes in life outcomes. Keep in mind that our careers are a complex system, and in complex systems, even the most simple changes can have dramatic outcomes.

The safer the environment, the more likely personal evolution is to truly take hold.

The hard reality of biology and evolution is that nearly all mutations kill us. Some we call the various forms of cancer; some we label other diseases. There are no guarantees against any of them, but the Spark Sequence is as close to total protection as you are ever likely to find. By breaking risk down into its component parts, we get the chance to navigate around each one separately while we build confidence that the variation in question will lead us in a positive new direction.

All of this works, but it also takes work.

And grit. And determination. And even courage. It requires gazing at a better horizon, along with daily thought and attention. The best things in life aren't free.

Every single person I interviewed for this book had a story to tell about buckling knees and weakening resolve. Sylvia Lagnado would go on to launch one of the most highly praised and admired ad campaigns in modern corporate history, but not before she looked down a darkening tunnel and wondered if the light at the end was a train headed her way.

Everyone I interviewed had an escape route planned in case things didn't work out. Even after she had secured a patent on the product that would make her a megamillionaire, Sara Blakely was ready to walk away from the struggle if no augury of success was forthcoming. On her way to becoming one of America's most highly esteemed leaders, Frances Hesselbein insisted that each new leadership role be temporary. I continued to look for work long after World50 had signed up its first client, and I even had a fat $50,000 sitting in my fledgling corporate account.

Everyone also came out on the other side of his or her leap stumbling like a person who had been living in a cave and was suddenly thrown into broad daylight. Jeff Gray had been a striving deal-maker all of his adult life. He knew that world cold. Yet in the weeks after he had finally made the commitment to his new life as an advocate for the dispossessed, he would often stop and look up at the gleaming office towers of

the big city and wonder what in the world people actually did
inside them.

Making the Leap Work for You

So, what can you do to launch your own career on a trajectory that might leave you dazed by where you once were and
energized as never before? It all begins with action. Here's the
starter kit:

- Work to find your strengths and passions, and once
  you have found your Primary Color, work to move in
  whatever direction it points you. This doesn't have to
  be earthshaking in itself. You don't need to quit your
  job or insist on a new office or title. Instead, simply
  think of one thing in the last year that you really loved
  at work, and then think of how you can incorporate
  more of that activity into your current role. Let your
  sense of fulfillment point you from there.
- Take a current idea, a value proposition for an existing
  or new product, or whatever else is already at hand, and
  run it through the big, selfless, and simple filter. Brain-
  storm big, selfless, and simple with your team. This is
  all about testing each idea, stretching it, uncovering the
  potential within it. Then take existing and new ideas
  about your own future and where you want your career
  trajectory to be taking you and run them through the
  same filter. If they fail to measure up, ask yourself how
  you can make them more of each.
- Start to spark. What great dream do you have? Does

it engage your strengths and passions? Does it pass the big, selfless, and simple test? If so, think of five totally risk-free actions you could take that would help you explore it. How can you gather more information? Is there any way to gain a brief experience, maybe through volunteering? And remember that even failed sparks have more value than never sparking at all. It's the movement that counts. The outcome will take care of itself.

Are, Should, and Could

What you *are* doing now is a matter of record. What you *should* be doing—what work is right for you, what career track will bring you the greatest fulfillment, what lily pad you ought to be looking at the world from, where your leap should be taking you—is utterly personal and singular. A million monkeys at a million word processors couldn't begin to scratch in print the surface of the possibilities.

What you *could* be doing is what this book is about.

What you *could* be doing is focusing on life-changing opportunities that offer a significant increase in your happiness combined with a high probability of success.

What you *could* be doing is making certain you are on the right journey: toward your Primary Color, in search of directions that will compel others to join and support you in your quest.

What you *could* be doing is sparking your way along a path that will allow you to test whatever myriad possibilities occur to you in pursuit of the ultimate combustion that will come when you find the one path that is right for you alone.

As I wrote at the start of this book, the journey is what matters. It's your chance to reimagine work, reignite potential, and make the leap from good to great. It's the action that holds real meaning. That's where the real clarity lies, where careers become callings.

That's where your future begins.

My Leap Journal—
Aristotle on a Lily Pad

Is my work the center of my life and identify? How closely aligned is my work identity to my ideal life identity?

What does it really mean to "have it all"?

If my life was absolutely perfect, how would it look?

What is missing in my life right now that is important to me?

How much money is enough? If I had more than enough, how would my goals change? Where I would spend my time? Would I simply move the finish line, or seek a different, higher purpose?

Would I be willing to take a less stressful (and less paying) job to be happier? To be closer to my true self?

What do I want to be remembered for?

What steps do I need to take tomorrow to ensure that the rest of my life will be all that I hope it can be?

· ACKNOWLEDGMENTS ·

There's a memorable scene in the movie *It's a Wonderful Life* when Jimmy Stewart's character, George Bailey, in complete despair, jumps off a bridge into the icy water below. That's a much different Leap than the one I advocate in this book, but George's plunge has a happy ending because, within moments, his guardian angel, Clarence, shows up to rescue his life. I know the feeling. During the earliest days of the launch of World 50, I stood on that bridge many a time. But I was fortunate enough to have my own guardian angel—in fact, I have a whole host of them.

Roger Fransecky believed in me when no one else did. He nudged, prodded, poked, and downright pushed me along when setbacks might have stopped me in my tracks. I cannot imagine anyone outside of my family having a more positive and significant impact on my life. You are a dear friend.

World 50 would have never have been possible without the tireless efforts of our early team. Elane Stock provided critical strategic thinking during the first months of existence. Jenn Green, magical Jenn Green, left a good, stable job to join me as employee number two and changed the outcome of our company and her life in the process. David Wilkie was valued partner from the very beginning, whose work ethic and intense love for the business dramatically impacted our success. Jeffrey Merrihue, Ellen Donovan, Laura Faulring, April Gardner, Lorraine Naga, Laurie Larsh, Leanne Anderson, Jennifer Newton, Arndt Oesterle, Carol Seymour, Larry Handen, Rosi Ware, Greg Welch, Lee Esler, Sir Martin Sorrel, Marcus Buckingham, Keith Ferrazzi, Mark Kaiser, Miles Nadal, Dean Crutchfield, Marc Mathieu, Courtenay Daniels, Allen Chan, Kathy Bremmer, Jim Citrin, Sam Pettway, David Daniel, Jennifer Potter-Brotman, David Kidder, Sean Seitzinger, Sharon Hall, John Yates, Ed Hirsch, Ken Bernhardt, Mark Toon, Bruce Barlag, Jim Davenport, Tony Robbins, Tim Ferriss, Scott Miller, Daniel Casse, David Niles and Peter Economy all provided critical and unexpected levels of support when it was needed most.

Justin Anthony, Sara Blakely, Mitch Free, Gardiner Garrard, Jon Carrol, Mark Monroe, Scott Geller, Brandyn Chapman, Mike Seckler, and Andy Levine—all members of my EO entrepreneur CEO forum—contributed incredible guidance and friendship throughout the growth and sale of my company, and the development of this book.

I would also like to thank World 50's many advisers and contributors, without whose trust and collaboration we could never have provided such a unique experience. These include Robert Redford, Bono, Lance Armstrong, Francis Ford Coppola, Sir John Major, Robert Dole, George Mitchell, Andre Aggassi, Jon Stewart, Magic Johnson, Russell Simmons,

Alan Greenspan, H. Norman Schwarzkopf, Dr. Mehmet Oz, Geoff Colvin, Stephen Colbert, Martha Stewart, Dr. Henry Kissinger, Ram Charan, Larry Bossidy, and Jim Kilts, among many others.

Turning such an ambitious project into an entertaining and readable book is rarely the work of an author alone. I would like to thank Howard Means, who was my partner in the creation of this book from the very beginning. His writing and editorial skills are unsurpassed, as is his ability to always know exactly what I am trying to say. I have rarely worked in such an enjoyable and effective collaboration, and it is my hope that we endeavor to partner on many projects in the future.

Kevin Small, Jayme Johnson, Mat Miller, Jane Wesman, John Saddington, Jonathan Bostic, Dr. Bill Brittain, Timothy Russell, Ward Binns, and Jeanette Bryce were all part of one of the most remarkable marketing and development teams any author has ever had the pleasure to work with.

Adrian Zackheim, Adrienne Schultz, Allison McLean, and the team at Penguin Group USA were extremely helpful in taking a good idea and turning it into a great project. Al Zuckerman represented me superbly, and I will always be grateful to Jane Wesman for introducing us.

Most of all, I must thank my wife, Lori, and our three wonderful children—Arden, Adam, and Laine. They supported me through the tough and uncertain trough of launching a start-up, into the hectic spiraling growth of World 50 and its eventual sale, and finally through the production and publication of this book. In so many ways, I stand on the shoulders of their support.

· INDEX ·

Ready to Start Your Leap?

Author Rick Smith has produced 5 FREE resources to help you do just that. These tools, inspired by *The Leap*, will help you put the book's ideas into practice.

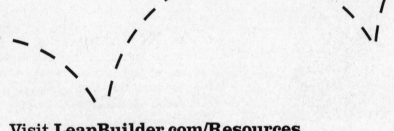

Visit LeapBuilder.com/Resources to download these **FREE** resources:

My Leap Journal
Preserve the pages of the book and download your own *My Leap Journal*.
One PDF with all the exercise questions from the book, all in one place!

The Leap Model
Want an easy reminder of the book's key concepts? Download this reference tool and hang it up near your desk.

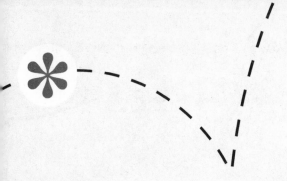

Escape the Now Trap

Need some encouragement and motivation to stay focused on your Leap? In this audio lesson, Rick Smith dispels the myths that too often keep us trapped in our current okay-but-average lives to propel us toward the extraordinary career we were meant to achieve.

Host a Leap Builder Party

Are you ready to take your own Leap? Getting there is easier (and more fun) with the support and encouragement of others discovering their own new paths. This resource provides everything you'll need to organize a successful night with friends or co-workers and get you moving toward your Leap.

Leap Interviews

See inspiring interviews with people featured in *The Leap*. Learn from others who have successfully made their own Leaps, as they delve deeper into the details of their own unique transitions.

Visit **LeapBuilder.com/Resources** to download these **FREE** resources.

Bring Rick Smith to Your Organization!

One of Rick Smith's primary missions is to help individuals improve their lives through their work, and in the process unlock latent productivity within organizations. A keynote speech can be a very effective way to introduce this mission into your organization, and motivate individuals to action.

Rick is currently speaking on the following topics:

The Leap
Can individuals jump to entirely new levels of productivity and success? Yes! Rick offers a fascinating and compelling framework for individuals to dramatically accelerate their impact in the workplace, unlock dormant potential, and achieve great things for themselves and their employers.

The 5 Patterns of Extraordinary Careers
Based on an extensive research study, this presentation reveals what factors allow employees to break from the crowd, dramatically increase their productivity and effectiveness, and unlock the true potential in their careers. Inspiring for employees, and an effective tool for employers.

For more information on inviting Rick to speak,
please visit **www.RickSmith.me**